General Studies Series

TIMBER CONSTRUCTION FOR DEVELOPING COUNTRIES

Applications and Examples

UNITED NATIONS INDUSTRIAL DEVELOPMENT ORGANIZATION

Vienna, 1995

ID/SER.O/10

UNIDO PUBLICATION
UNIDO.92.10.E
ISBN 92-1-106296-9

Explanatory notes

AITC	American Institute of Timber Construction
AS	Australian Standard
CSIRO	Commonwealth Scientific and Industrial Research Organization
emc	equilbrium moisture content
fsp	fibre paturation point
ILO	International Labour Organisation
MOE	modulus of elasticity
MOR	modulus of rupture
TEW	Timber Engineering Workshop
UNIDO	United Nations Industrial Development Organization

PREFACE

Whether grown in a particular country or not, wood is a virtually universal material that is familiar to people all over the world. It is used for many purposes but principally for construction, furniture, packaging and other specialized uses such as transmission poles, railway ties, matches and household articles. The United Nations Industrial Development Organization (UNIDO), which was established in 1967 to assist developing countries in their efforts to industrialize, has the responsibility within the United Nations system for assisting in the development of secondary woodworking industries and has carried out this responsibility since its inception at the national, regional and interregional levels by means of projects both large and small. UNIDO also assists by preparing manuals on topics that are common to the woodworking sectors of most countries.*

The lectures presented at the Timber Engineering Workshop (TEW), held from 2 to 20 May 1983 at Melbourne, Australia, are part of the continuing efforts of UNIDO to help engineers and specifiers appreciate the role that wood can play as a structural material. Collected in the form of 38 chapters, these lectures have been entitled Timber Construction for Developing Countries, which forms part of the General Studies Series. Twelve of the chapters make up this fifth volume of the collection, Applications and Examples. The TEW was organized by UNIDO with the cooperation of the Commonwealth Scientific and Industrial Research Organization (CSIRO) and was funded by a contribution made under the Australian Government's vote of aid to the United Nations Industrial Development Fund. Administrative support was provided by the Department of Industry and Commerce of the Australian Government. The remaining lectures (chapters), which cover a wide range of subjects, including case studies, are contained in four additional volumes, as shown in the table of contents.

Following the pattern established for other specialized technical training courses in this sector, notably the course on furniture and joinery and that on criteria for the selection of woodworking machinery,** the lectures were complemented by visits to sites and factories, discussion sessions and work assignments carried out by small groups of participants.

It is hoped that the publication of these lectures will lead to the greater use of timber as a structural material to help satisfy the tremendous need in the developing countries for domestic, agricultural, industrial and commercial buildings and for structures such as bridges. It is also hoped that the lectures will be of use to teachers in training institutes as well as to engineers and architects in public and private practice.

Readers should note that the examples cited often reflect Australian conditions and thus may not be wholly applicable to developing countries,

---

*These activities are described more fully in the booklet UNIDO for Industrialization: Wood Processing and Wood Products (PI/78).

**The lectures for these two courses were collected and published as Furniture and Joinery Industries for Developing Countries (United Nations publication, Sales No. E.88.III.E.7) and Technical Criteria for the Selection of Woodworking Machines (UNIDO publication, Sales No. 92.1.E).

despite the widespread use of the Australian timber stress grading and strength grouping systems and despite the wide range of conditions encountered on the Australian subcontinent. Moreover, it must be remembered that some of the technology that is mentioned as having been new at the time of the Workshop (1983) may since then have been further developed. Similarly, standards and grading systems that were just being developed or introduced at that time have now become accepted. Readers should also note that the lectures were usually complemented by slides and other visual aids and by informal comments by the lecturer, which gave added depth of coverage.

CONTENTS*

*For the reader's convenience the contents of the four complementary volumes are also given here.

Figures

Introduction to Wood and Timber Engineering
(ID/SER.0/6)

  I. Forest products resources
     W. E. Hillis

 II. Timber engineering and its application in developing
     countries
     John G. Stokes

III. Wood, the material
     W. E. Hillis

 IV. Mechanical properties of wood
     Leslie D. Armstrong

  V. Conversion of timber
     Mervyn W. Page

 VI. Seasoning of structural timber
     F. J. Christensen

Structural Timber and Related Products
(ID/SER.0/7)

  I. Characteristics of structural timber
     Robert H. Leicester

 II. Structural grading of timber
     William G. Keating

III. Proof grading of timber
     Robert H. Leicester

INTRODUCTION

Many developing countries are fortunate in having good resources of timber, but virtually all countries make considerable use of wood and wood products, whether home-grown or imported, for housing and other buildings, in both structural and non-structural applications, as well as for furniture and cabinet work and specialized uses. Although wood is a familiar material, it is all too often misunderstood or not fully appreciated since it exists in a great variety of types and qualities.

Some species, such as teak, oak and pine, are well known almost everywhere while others, such as beech, eucalyptus, acacia, mahogany and rosewood, are known primarily in particular regions. Still others, notably the merantis, lauans and keruing, which come from South-East Asia, have only recently been introduced to widespread use. Very many more species exist and are known locally and usually used to good purpose by those in the business. Also, plantations are now providing an increasing volume of wood.

The use of timber for construction is not new and, in fact, has a very long tradition. In many countries this tradition has unfortunately given way to the use of other materials - notably, concrete, steel and brick - whose large industries have successfully supported the development of design information and the teaching of methods for engineering them. This has not been so much the case for timber, despite considerable efforts by some research and development institutions in countries where timber and timber-framed construction have maintained a strong position. Usually the building methods are based on only a few well-known coniferous (softwood) species and a limited number of standard sizes and grades. For these, ample design aids exist, and relatively few problems are encountered by the very many builders involved.

Recent developments in computer-aided design and in factory-made components and fully prefabricated houses have led to better quality control and a decreased risk of site problems. Other modern timber engineering developments have enabled timber to be used with increasing confidence for an ever wider range of structures. This has been especially so in North America, Western Europe, Australia and New Zealand.

UNIDO feels that an important means of transferring this technology is the organization of specialized training courses that introduce engineers, architects and specifiers to the subject and draw their attention to the advantages of wood, as well as its disadvantages and potential problem areas, and also to reference sources. In this way, for particular projects or structures, wood will be fairly considered in competition with other materials and used when appropriate. Comparative costs, aesthetic considerations and tradition must naturally be taken into account in the context of each country and project, but it is hoped that the publication of these lectures will lead those involved to a rational approach to the use of wood in construction and remove some of the misunderstandings and misapprehensions all too often associated with this ancient yet modern material.

I. SPECIFICATION OF TIMBER FOR STRUCTURAL USE

William G. Keating*

Introduction

The value of timber as a structural material has been verified by centuries of use. However, it could have established its reputation more economically if the relationship between quality and usefulness had been more completely understood. Nowadays it is essential that the costs of both erection and maintenance are contained within competitive limits. This can be done by three means:

(a) Keeping material quantities to the minimum necessary;

(b) Designing for adequate safety and performance;

(c) Avoiding costly maintenance or premature replacement.

Another concern for the community as a whole is the depletion of the world's finite resources. In this regard, timber has a definite advantage over other materials because it is renewable. Still, this is no excuse for wasteful practices.

Obviously, correct specification is one way of overcoming the above problems. Most countries have established national standards that recommend methods of specifying materials and their correct use. Because of their importance, timber and its derived products are usually well catered for, but this does not necessarily mean that such standards are always used or even well understood.

The development of standards generally, and in particular those relating to timber, has been a product of improved communications and closer international cooperation. In the past, timber standards were often prepared, written and promulgated by people who wanted to sell the local product but did not pay sufficient attention to the long-term reputation of a vital raw material. Gradually, standards around the world have tended to become themselves standardized. This approach has succeeded to a much greater degree than many thought possible even a few years ago. It is obvious that through these developments, the technology transfer process has been enhanced considerably and that any country, particularly a developing one, is able to take advantage of advances made in another country. Engineers who saw this happening in the newer materials such as steel and concrete looked for the same in timber and, depending on the particular situation, either exerted their influence on the timber standards committees or turned to the other materials.

To the specifier, standards are particularly useful, even essential, but they may need to be added to or substracted from to make a complete specification. For timber, this implies an understanding of its characteristics, particularly its limitations as well as its special properties.

___

*An officer of CSIRO, Division of Chemical and Wood Technology, Melbourne.

The following is an example of specification writing that was common some years ago and shows the completely unrealistic approach that often prevailed:

"Scantling shall be the best of its kind cut from mature, hill-grown trees felled during the winter. It shall be perfectly straight and out of winding, die-square, bone dry and free from heart, sap and all defects."

Modern day standards more closely match the needs of the user with the availability of the material.

A. Basic working stresses

Previous papers have shown how timber may be graded for structural purposes and how a basic working stress may be derived. As this is the figure from which the engineer starts the design process, it follows that the first requirement he or she specifies is the stress grade of the desired timber. In Australia, stress grading entails the classification of a piece of timber for structural purposes by means of either visual or mechanical grading to indicate the basic working stresses and stiffnesses to be used for structural design purposes. The stress grade is designated in a form such as F7, which would indicate that the basic working stress in bending was approximately 7 MPa.

B. Timber identification

In many situations, the engineer, provided he or she is satisfied as to the stress grade, is not too concerned about the identity of the timber. However, there are also many cases where positive species identification is essential, at least in so far as a strength group classification is concerned. One such situation applies when there exists a biological hazard. To remove the hazard, the engineer may need to specify one or more of the following:

(a) The use of timbers treated with preservatives. There are three possible approaches:

(i) The timber is surrounded by a complete envelope of preserved timber of such depth that provides for post-treatment surface checking and minor damage during fabrication. This procedure is carried out after all cutting, drilling, notching, machining etc., has been done;

(ii) The timber is treated through its full depth with adequate retentions of preservative;

(iii) Only the susceptible sapwood is treated against Lyctus attack;

(b) The use of naturally durable heartwood species that can be identified on site, for protection against fungal attack only;

(c) The provision of adequate ventilation against fungal (decay) attack;

(d) The use of soil poisoning and/or mechanical barriers such as "ant" capping against termites.

In (a) and (b) above, species identification is essential.

For the design of timber structures, it may be necessary to use unseasoned timber if the member cross-sections are so large as to make it uneconomic to specify dry timber. This is not necessarily a problem, because construction techniques are available to minimize the effects of shrinkage; here again, however, species or species group identification is important in order to predict the likely performance. The use of hardwoods tends to exacerbate the situation, for their total volumetric shrinkage is usually much higher than that of softwoods and the differential percentage shrinkage in the tangential and radial directions is also higher. Here, too, it may be of some importance to know the identity of those pieces that could be subject to the abnormal form of shrinkage known as collapse. Standard texts list those species that are known to be susceptible, but identification is necessary.

C. Dimensions and tolerances

It is important that there is no cause for ambiguity when stating dimensions and tolerances. In Australia, lineal metres or cubic metres are the units of measurement for length and volume, respectively, and the cross-sections are referred to in millimetres. The convention that is being encouraged is to specify cross-section, number of pieces and lengths in that order, e.g. 100 x 50 60/2.4, where 100 x 50 indicates the required cross-section in millimetres and 60/2.4 indicates 60 pieces each 2.4 m long. For tolerances, the designer should make it clear to the supplier, usually by quoting the appropriate standard, that he or she understands, for example, that a negative tolerance on cross-section is permissible. Usually this applies only to unseasoned sawn timber. For dressed or seasoned timber, there is normally no negative tolerance. These points and the conditions relating to length tolerances are usually spelt out in the standard.

D. Standards

The value of standards becomes obvious when ordering timber. By quoting the stress grade, the identity of the species (to the precision necessary) and the number of the standard to which the timber is produced, a considerable amount of information is conveyed in a very small space. When that is combined with, say, a timber engineering code, the intentions of the designer and the responsibilities of the supplier are quite clear.

If no standard exists, it is normal practice to examine standards from other countries and modify them where necessary to suit local conditions. As can be imagined, this is not very satisfactory. If even this is not possible and trained graders are not available, some simple rules, combined with a minimum density clause, may be satisfactory. Such an approach would need to be conservative, but it could allow timber to be used.

E. Equilibrium moisture content

When structures or elements are to be fabricated with seasoned timber, the designer should ascertain the average equilibrium moisture content for the environment in which the structures or elements are to be erected. He or she should then specify that the timber used shall have a moisture content at the time of fabrication within 3 per cent of this average value.

Wood exposed to an atmosphere containing moisture in the form of water vapour will come, in time, to a steady moisture content condition, called the equilibrium moisture content. This steady moisture state depends on the relative humidity, the temperature of the surrounding air and the drying conditions that it has previously undergone. It fluctuates with changes in

one or both of these atmospheric conditions. Such changes produce corresponding changes in the dimensions of wood. To minimize the extent of such movement, it is desirable to install timber at a moisture content mid-way between
the extremes it is likely to reach in service. Between 12 and 14 per cent is
an average moisture content, but it could be higher in tropical areas or considerably lower in locations such as central Australia or indoors in
air-conditioned buildings.

F. Corrosion

Corrosion may occur in metal connectors used under moist conditions and
under certain atmospheric conditions such as might be encountered in marine
environments, certain factories or near chlorinated water. Condensation in
the roofs of heated buildings will also encourage corrosion. Some water-borne
preservatives may, under moist conditions, corrode unprotected metal work.
The designer must ascertain if such hazardous conditions are likely to be
encountered and ensure that the appropriate precautions are taken.

On the other hand, wood itself does not corrode, which makes it a most
useful material to specify for use in a corrosive environment.

G. Preservative type

It is not sufficient for the designer to specify simply that the timber
members be treated with preservatives, should that be necessary. The preservative type must also be specified. Oil, water and light organic solvent
types each have their own advantages and limitations, so that in order to make
the correct choice some attempt to acquire the necessary background information is required.

H. Transport and erection

The overstressing of timber members during transport and erection should
be carefully avoided. Special care is necessary to avoid distortion in hoist-
ing framed arches, trusses, portal frames and the like from the horizontal to
the vertical position. For this reason, the designer should indicate lifting
points or methods of lifting on the design.

I. Built-up members

Often it is not possible to obtain solid timber members of sufficiently
large cross-section or length to suit a particular need. This does not preclude the use of timber, as large members may be formed from much smaller
pieces. However, for engineered structures this is a specialized technique
and one that needs a first-class quality control system. For this reason, if
it is designed to use members such as glue-laminated beams or nail-laminated
components, the designer must seek guidance from an appropriate standard and
order from a well-known and reputable firm.

Simple members may be fabricated on-site, but close supervision is
usually necessary.

J. Storage on site

Unless specifically designed for the purpose, timber components and
structural elements should not be exposed to high humidity, and all materials
and assemblies in storage should be protected against exposure to the weather,
wetting, damage, decay and insect attack. Adequate ventilation of the stock
must be provided.

K. Inspection on site

It is not sufficient for the designer to just write the specification, even if it does cover all the aspects already mentioned. He or she must provide for a system of regular, on-site check inspections. This implies that there is someone present, such as the site engineer or foreman, who is at least familiar with the standards quoted in the contract, any special conditions and the way in which the checks should be made.

For example, the specification of dry timber would normally indicate that this was critical to the performance of the structure. In structural members, if green timber is supplied in place of the specified dry timber, failure is possible, excessive deflection is probable and end splitting may occur, rendering the jointing devices inoperative. For these reasons, it is good practice to have available at the site a moisture meter and someone who knows how to use it. Similar care must be taken with preservative-treated timber and to ensure conformance to the grading rules. Branding is not always a cause for complete assurance, but it is a useful safeguard and indicates the supplier will back his product, which is often why it was specified in the first place. For this reason, checks are necessary to ensure that the agreed branding has been done in the correct manner and frequency.

L. Summary

Timber is a well-proven structural material, but its familiarity often leads to its misuse. Modern technology has enabled us to specify timber in much more economic (i.e. smaller) sizes over a wider range of conditions than in the past, but at the same time the need for close attention to specification detail has been markedly increased.

Bibliography

Panshin, A. J. and G. de Zeeuw. Textbook of wood technology. 3. ed. New York, McGraw-Hill, 1970.

Standards Association of Australia. Draft revision of SAA timber engineering code. Sydney, 1982.

Timber Promotion Council. Understanding Victorian structural hardwood. Melbourne, Australia, 1982.

II. PLYWOOD IN CONCRETE FORMWORK

Kevin J. Lyngcoln*

This lecture/chapter was based on a manual of the same title by Mr. Lyngcoln. The manual is not reproduced here; however, it may be obtained from the Plywood Association of Australia Ltd.** The following passage from the foreword to the Manual gives an idea of its scope and purpose:

"Concrete in Australia over the past few decades has developed into one of the most used materials in the building industry. Its ability to be moulded into a great variety of shapes, its ability to accept a wide range of surface finishes and its inherent strength and durability provide designers with an extremely versatile design medium. The development of "off-form" finishes in particular has given architects yet another means of creating building facades in economic and aesthetically pleasing forms.

"The success of concrete as a visual material depends in no small measure, however, on the quality of the formwork that moulds it into the desired shape, and in particular on the quality of the form face. Plywood has become established as a major material for this purpose.

"Production of "off-form" finishes imposes much tighter limits on concrete formwork. In particular, water absorption of the form face, joint sealing and deflection under load are critical. Whilst in most cases the structural strength of formwork systems is more than adequate, the control of deflection and the sealing of joints are sometimes not given the same attention and the concrete finish suffers accordingly.

"This Manual ... addresses itself to these problems, provides the building industry with efficient design methods and suggests effective details to ensure that the best performance is obtained from concrete. Consideration is given also, in the section on formwork pressure, to the effects on formwork design of modern trends which involve more workable concretes, greater rates of concrete placement and emphasis on the overall speed of construction. Each of these tends to impose additional loads and pressures on the formwork and demand more accurate designs to ensure that strength, deflection and sealing requirements are met."

The determination of concrete pressures on horizontal and vertical formwork, the estimation of vertical rates of pour and beam design are discussed in the first section of the Manual. A section on the characteristics of formwork plywood covers its advantages, the properties that affect structural performance, control of the surface finish, standard dimensions and

---

*Engineer, Plywood Association of Australia Ltd.
**P.O. Box 8, Newstead, Queensland 4006, Australia.

tolerances and the marking of plywood for formwork. Another section describes the structural properties of formwork plywood: basic working stresses, section properties and allowable concrete pressures.

The Manual contains 20 figures and 8 tables. Its three appendices address
the calculation of section properties and of allowable concrete pressures and
also present examples of typical formwork using plywood designs.

III. TIMBER STRUCTURES: DETAILING FOR DURABILITY

Leslie D. Armstrong*

Introduction

Building materials will deteriorate extensively in the absence of good principles for the construction, use and maintenance of buildings and other structures. Where high rainfall, high humidity, extensive insolation and strong winds prevail, materials can decay rapidly without proper emphasis on good practice.

The same weathering factors operate in the tropics as in temperate regions, although the considerable variation in intensity make some factors insignificant and others important. Some processes of degradation, particularly attack by biological agents, are likely to be hastened by the uniform, optimum temperatures that are experienced towards the equator, while some physical effects, such as those that result from dimensional change, are promoted in hot, arid regions where there are low night-time temperatures.

Skilled designers attempt to achieve the best performance in buildings by the selection of durable materials, the exercise of good principles of construction and workmanship and the provision for proper treatment and maintenance to increase durability. These important approaches are never fully achieved, even in large cities where materials and skilled labour are abundant; usually they are only partially achieved in smaller cities and towns in remote regions where materials and skilled tradesmen are in short supply.

The behaviour of timber in service is affected by environmental and biological factors that vary in their influence depending on the conditions of exposure. Usually, the worst conditions are those of outdoor exposure, because variations in climate are large and have the greatest impact; however, severe conditions may also occur indoors owing to hazardous artificial environments or poor techniques of construction.

A. Timber used indoors

The major problems associated with the deterioration of structural timbers used indoors are usually due to excessive amounts of liquid water in direct contact with the timber, excessive amounts of water vapour in the atmosphere, excessive fluctuations in the moisture content of the wood, extremes of temperature or the presence of chemical fumes. When the moisture content of wood exceeds about 25 per cent, based on its oven-dry weight, biological decay due to bacteria or fungi may occur. The effects intensify as the temperature increases. Should the moisture content of the wood fluctuate appreciably with changes in atmospheric conditions, which may happen in industrial buildings, excessive amounts of swelling and shrinkage may result, and this can cause severe stressing and degradation of the timber and associated joints. Checking or splitting of the wood surface may also occur,

---

*Formerly an officer of CSIRO, Division of Building Research, Melbourne.

with bacteria or fungi developing in the checks and causing the wood to decay. In tropical climates, high relative humidities persist for extensive periods. To inhibit biological attack in timber in these climates, it is usually necessary to apply preservative chemicals and protective films to the surfaces of members and to ensure the adequate ventilation of air spaces. There is also an increased hazard from water penetration and flooding of structures, which requires proper shielding and drainage systems to shed water and prevent retention.

Although timber in service is rarely affected by chemical fumes, the metal fasteners commonly used in timber joints may corrode unless they have been treated to withstand specific chemicals.

B. Timber used outdoors

When used externally, timber may be partially or fully exposed to the weather, and its moisture content may reach undesirable values or may fluctuate widely due to exposure to the sun, rain, snow or wind. In some cases, harmful chemicals may come in contact with the timber and joints. The orientation of the structure should be considered at the planning stage to reduce the exposure of vulnerable components. Protective treatments consisting of durable surface coatings or penetrating chemicals may have to be used to help the timber to resist damaging agents or to inhibit moisture changes. These treatments assist in keeping swelling stresses to a minimum and reduce the incidence of biological decay. Consideration should be given to the method of assembly of timber components: in so far as possible, water should not be able to pond on surfaces nor enter the joints, and any water that does intrude should be able to drain away. Moisture should also be prevented from diffusing into wood from porous media, such as soil or concrete, by avoiding direct contact. Continued observation and maintenance will also be needed during the life of the structure, as is the case with all structures and materials.

The methods of providing physical protection for timber structures and components fall into two categories, shielding and structural detailing.

C. Shielding methods

Structural timber exposed on the outside of a building may be shielded from the weather by natural and/or artificial systems of protection. By carefully selecting the type and location of trees and shrubs, timber walls and exposed structural timbers may be substantially protected from the wind and rain, thus inhibiting the entry of water and reducing excessive fluctuations in moisture content (figure 1). Shielding from the sun is also achieved with shrubs, which not only protect the exposed timber but also benefit the internal environment of a building by shading the walls and windows. Careful selection of the species of trees and shrubs will ensure an acceptable degree of shielding for the building.

The trees and shrubs must be far enough from the building and far enough apart so that the foliage does not constitute a source of moisture or inhibit the flow of air adjacent to the walls; otherwise the moisture content of exposed timber may reach detrimental levels. The trees must be of species that will not topple onto the buildings during wind storms. Further, the root growth and moisture requirements must also be considered so that there is no damage to the foundations of the buildings from excessive moisture changes in the soil or the intrusion of roots. Botanists and experienced nurserymen should be consulted during tree selection, planting and landscaping.

Figure 1. Vegetation intercepts sun, wind and rain but allows
air circulation near the building to inhibit moisture build-up

Where it is not convenient to use trees for shielding, artificial systems
may be installed to achieve a similar purpose. Roof overhangs, shading
devices and screen walls or fences can be constructed of decorative and
durable materials to provide protection against the elements, to assist indoor
temperature control and to enhance the architecture (figures 2 and 3). Practical experience throughout the world has demonstrated the extremely valuable
contribution made by shielding systems in prolonging the life of exposed
building materials.

Figure 2. Architectural overhang intercepts sun and rain

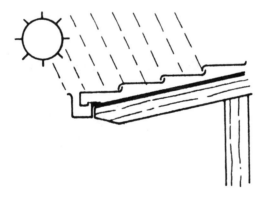

Figure 3. Architectural screen wall and pergola intercepts sun,
wind and rain but allows air circulation near the building

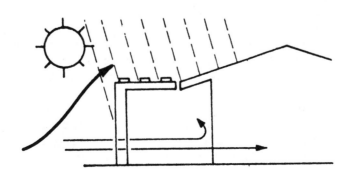

Other methods of shielding consist of applying caps or flashing directly to the surfaces of exposed timber members to prevent water from lodging on surfaces and to divert it away from the members (figures 4 and 5).

Figure 4. Flashing sheds water and protects the upper and end surfaces of the beam. The shield does not fold under to the lower surface because the water could be trapped there

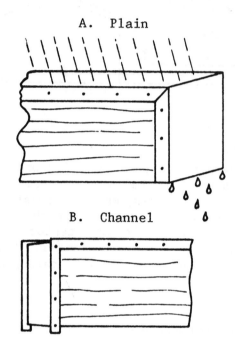

Figure 5. Caps protect the end grain

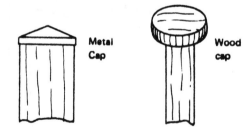

Improperly designed shielding systems may accentuate rather than alleviate the degradation of timber by trapping water that has leaked into the shields. A shield or cap should cover only the exposed surface that requires protection, leaving adequate ventilation and drainage of the remaining surfaces, especially the lower surfaces, so that moisture will not be retained on the timber, causing prolonged wetting and subsequent biological decay.

The end-grain surfaces of wood need special treatment with respect to shielding and sealing. Moisture is gained and lost more readily through end-grain than through side-grain surfaces. The checking of end-grain surfaces may become severe because of differences in swelling in the tangential and radial directions, relative to the growth rings, and biological decay may develop in the open checks. Shields of the types already described may be formed to protect end-grain surfaces, and a variety of sealing paints and films can also be applied. Some other treatments have proved successful in inhibiting the deterioration of end-grain surfaces: shaping the ends of members to reduce exposure and to encourage water run off (figure 6), machining a groove into the face or attaching a strip to provide a drip bead, or subdividing the large end face of a member into a number of small sections by means of deep saw kerfs to relieve swelling stresses and reduce checking (figure 7).

Figure 6.   Shaping encourages water run-off and decreases the exposure of the end grain to sun and rain

Figure 7.   Saw kerfs 3-5 mm wide and 20 mm deep relieve swelling stresses and reduce checking

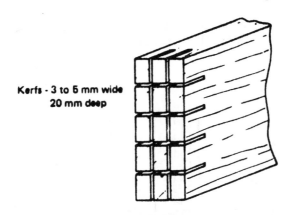

Kerfs - 3 to 5 mm wide
20 mm deep

Timber that is totally immersed in water will not decay. However, when a structural member, such as a pile, is partially immersed in water and partially exposed to air, the wood may degrade at the water-line unless protective methods are applied to reduce moisture content fluctuations and to inhibit checking and subsequent decay. One method of treatment is to apply a bandage containing preservative to the section at the water-line.

D. Structural detailing

When timber components are joined or brought into contact with other structural members or materials, care must be taken to avoid the entry of water and, more importantly, to avoid trapping water in the joint. The shaping, caulking and flashing of timber members can encourage the drainage of water away from the joints and also inhibit the entry of water. Grooving and drilling the faces of members can encourage the drainage of water from inside joints where leakage may be present. The transfer of moisture from another porous medium, e.g. soil or concrete, to timber should be prevented, and the design of the joint should allow easy access for the application of mainte-nance treatments, especially to end-grain surfaces. Where metal shoes or fittings are used to support the ends of members they should not enclose the

member or encourage the trapping of water. If green timbers are used in construction, the joints, fasteners and support fittings must be selected to
accommodate the subsequent shrinkage of the timber and permit maintenance.
Similarly, where excessive moisture content fluctuations are expected, the
inevitable dimensional changes must be provided for. Several examples of good
structural detailing are shown in figures 8-12.

Figure 8.   Isolation of a wood column from a wet
source using a steel dowel

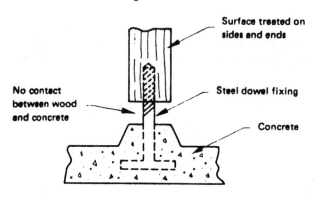

Figure 9.   Isolation of a wood column using a steel plate
and a bituminous pad

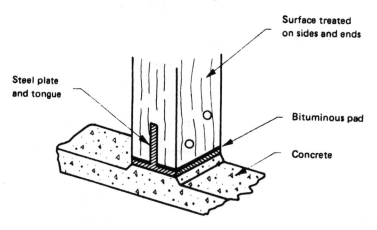

Figure 10.   Isolation and shielding

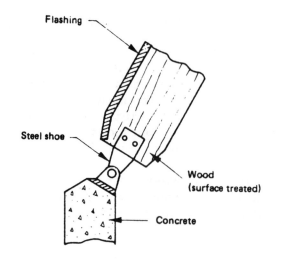

Figure 11. One method of support for a spaced column

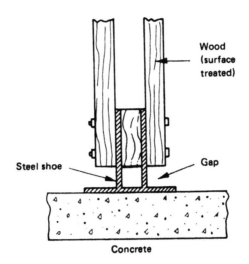

Figure 12. Alternative method of support for a spaced column

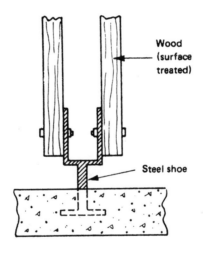

IV. USE OF GREEN TIMBER IN STRUCTURES

Leslie D. Armstrong*

Wood is a hygroscopic material that gains and loses water with variations in the moisture content of the environment in which it is used. Because the diffusion of moisture in wood is a rate process, there is a time lag between the variation of the moisture content of wood and the changes in atmospheric conditions. Moisture gradients develop below the surface of the wood, and severe distortions may occur in some timber components.

In service, timber may be fully immersed in water, with the result that its moisture content remains constantly high. Alternatively, it may be exposed to a variety of natural, controlled or widely variable artificial environments in which the moisture contents remain steady or fluctuate over a considerable range. The moisture content of wood varies in accordance with the surrounding conditions and, given sufficient time, it equilibrates with a particular environment, i.e. the moisture content of the wood reaches a steady value that is related to the moisture content of the surrounding air. In most countries, the moisture content levels of timber vary according to season. In Melbourne, the moisture content of wood used under shelter varies from about 10 to 15 per cent, based on the oven-dry weight of the wood, over the course of a year.

Wood in the tree contains water in two forms: free water, contained in the hollow lumen of the wood cell, and chemically bound water, contained in the wood tissue in the cell wall. As wood dries, the free water is first removed from the cell lumen to the surface of the wood, where it evaporates. The moisture content of the wood following removal of the free water is approximately 30 per cent, based on oven-dry weight, and is referred to as the fibre saturation point (fsp), as the cell wall remains saturated with bound water. As drying proceeds below this moisture content, the bound water diffuses from the cell wall to the external surfaces of the wood and evaporates until the moisture content of the wood is in equilibrium with that of the surrounding air. This moisture content level is known as the equilibrium moisture content of the sample (emc). In Melbourne, the emc ranges from about 10 to 15 per cent in timber exposed to ambient conditions and protected from direct rain and sun.

The loss of free water from the cell lumens of wood has little effect on the physical properties, except that in some species of hardwood a severe form of abnormal lateral shrinkage, known as collapse, can occur and cause extensive distortions and dimensional changes in the timber. Changes in cross-section of up to about 8 per cent of the original dimensions can occur with cell wall collapse in some species. Precautions must be taken when such timbers are used for construction.

---

*Formerly an officer of CSIRO, Division of Building Research, Melbourne.

The loss of bound water from the cell wall during the drying of timber below the fsp affects the mechanical and physical properties of the wood considerably. An important phenomenon that accompanies moisture change below the fsp is that of shrinkage and swelling of the lateral dimensions of wood as moisture is desorbed and adsorbed. Shrinkage parallel or tangential to the growth rings is much greater than shrinkage in the radial direction, sometimes twice as great. Shrinkage along the grain of wood is of little or no practical significance. In softwoods, depending on species, the original lateral dimensions can shrink up to about 6 per cent during drying from the fsp down to a typical air-dry condition of 12 per cent moisture content. In hardwoods, the lateral dimensions may shrink up to 10 per cent under similar conditions.

Apart from allowing for the shrinkage and swelling, or "working", of dry timber that may occur when the moisture content fluctuates with climatic changes, special attention must be paid to the greater changes in dimension that accompany the drying of initially green timber in service. This is particularly important with joints in timber components.

Obviously, furniture and joinery timbers should be dried to a moisture content equal to the mean of the range anticipated in practice, whether they are to be exposed to natural ambient conditions or artificially generated conditions. Structural timbers installed in the dry state should be treated in a similar manner. Timbers used over a short duration, e.g. for form-work, in extreme conditions may need surface treatment and protection to inhibit moisture changes and associated dimension changes.

Structural timber is frequently used in the green condition, as cut from freshly felled trees, because of the difficulties encountered in the seasoning of structural sizes, the high costs and delays experienced in seasoning and the problems encountered in nailing dry timber of many species. The problems that can arise when structural timbers shrink in reaction to extensive moisture content change are many and varied and sometimes give timber a bad name. Usually, however, these problems are the result of thoughtlessness or carelessness on the part of the designer or builder who fails to provide for the well-established shrinkage behaviour of construction timbers. Some of the common problems encountered in practice and the precautions needed in construction methods to reduce the detrimental effects of shrinkage are described next.

When initially green structural timbers of similar shrinkage characteristics are lapped or spliced using nails, bolts or connector rings and the direction of the wood fibres (grain of the wood) is disposed in the same direction in all timber members, as shown in figure 13, no restraints or splitting of the wood can occur between parallel rows of fasteners. However, bolt holes in the green timber must be drilled 1-2 mm oversize, depending upon the species and bolt diameter; otherwise splitting will occur in the grain direction adjacent to the holes when the hole diameter becomes smaller across the grain with shrinkage of the timber. In hardwoods, tangential shrinkage may amount to 15 per cent during drying from the green to the air-dry state, and in softwoods the shrinkage may reach 6 per cent. Bolts need retightening at intervals as the timber shrinks in thickness, and it is essential to use the correct size of washers under bolt heads and nuts to avoid crushing the timber and to keep bearing stresses within safe limits.

Figure 13. Shrinkage in a timber joint. No restraints occur between
fasteners in timbers of similar shrinkage properties and of similar
grain direction. For bolts, drill holes 1-2 mm oversize

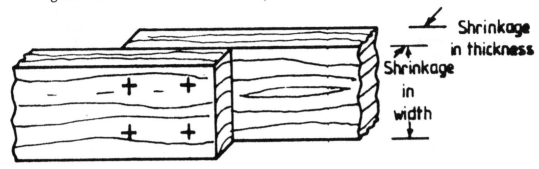

When the shrinkage characteristics of lapped or spliced green timbers are
very different or when the relative directions of the grain in adjacent
members may cause significantly different shrinkage effects across a joint,
staggering the fasteners in adjacent rows, as shown in figures 14 and 15, will
often alleviate splitting during shrinkage.

Figure 14.   Staggered fasteners joining green timbers of
different shrinkage properties

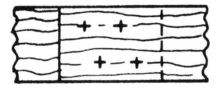

Figure 15.   Staggered fasteners joining green timbers of
different grain direction

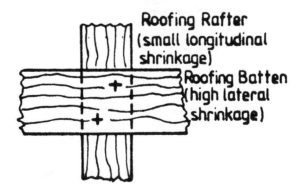

Steel plates are often used to splice green timber members butted
together at their ends. When the joint is formed using a single row of bolts
or screws along the length of the members, as shown in figure 16, no restraints occur across the joint provided the bolt holes are drilled oversize in

the timber. However, when two or more rows of fasteners are used in such an assembly, as shown in figure 17, alternate rows of holes in the steel plates must be slotted laterally to allow for the displacement of the bolts or screws across the splice plates as the green timber members shrink. Similar treatment may be needed when metal straps or angle brackets are used adjacent to green timber members (figure 18). The bolts or screws should be tightened regularly while the timber is shrinking.

Figure 16. Timber/steel plate assembly with single row of bolts.
Drill holes in the steel to suit the bolts. Drill holes
in the timber 1-2 mm oversize

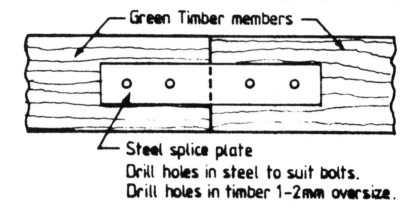

Figure 17. Timber/steel plate assembly with two or more rows
of bolts or screws

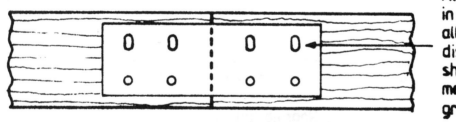

Built-up timber beams and trusses are often constructed of green hardwood members and webs or gussets of plywood, hardboard or galvanized iron. The common practice is to use two or more rows of nails, staples or rivets, as far apart as possible. This is satisfactory for small beam flanges or truss members but not for members 10 cm or more deep because the green members shrink and the gussets do not. As a result, the gusset is damaged, the fasteners are overstrained or the timber members are split. The correct practice is to use the minimum number of rows of nails or rivets, to space the rows as close together as permissible, to group the fasteners along the centre lines of the members and to stagger the fasteners in adjacent rows (figure 19).

Figure 18. Slotted holes should be provided in metal fittings
to allow for shrinkage of the adjacent timber

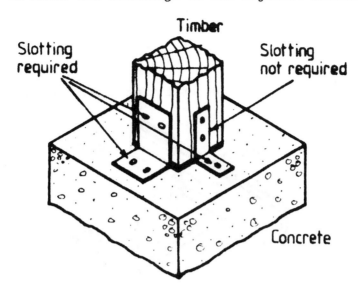

Figure 19. Reducing shrinkage problems in built-up components

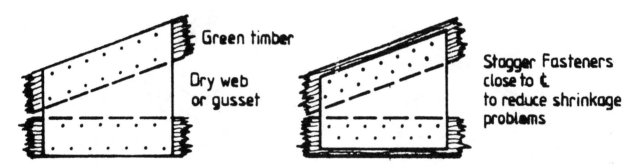

When green hardwood purlins are attached to wooden cleats as shown in
figure 20, trouble will occur in two places. The purlins and upper chords
will shrink in their depth whereas the cleats will not shrink in their
length. When the purlins shrink, they will no longer rest on the top chord of
the truss but will hang from the bolts attaching them to the cleats. When the
top chord shrinks, the two fastenings, either bolts or nails, will be forced
closer together and this may cause the cleat to split or break the joint.
Either way, the cleat is likely to become ineffective. Three more satisfactory purlin fixtures are shown in figure 21.

Figure 20. Poor fixing of green timber members

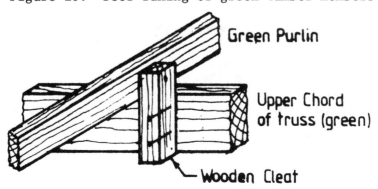

The nails or bolts attaching the purlin should be placed as close as practicable to the lower side of the purlin. If two bolts or nails are needed at each point of fixing of the purlin, these should not be placed in line across the depth of the purlin, as this will probably cause it to split. Figure 21 shows a simple strap hanger for the purlin.

Figure 21.   Improved methods of fixing green timber members

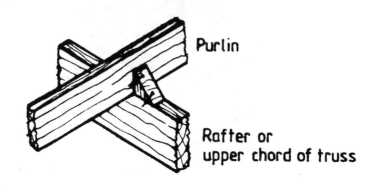

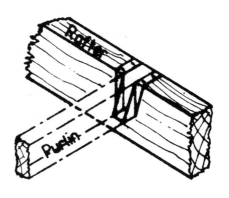

Floors, decks and verandahs are sometimes constructed of green timber joists that are supported on brickwork at one end and a green timber beam at the other end. The beam, in turn, is supported on steel or timber posts, as shown in figure 22. Shrinkage in the depth of the green timber beam may exceed 25 mm in a typical case using hardwood, causing this amount of mis-alignment in the floor. The problem may be solved by using similar support beams at each end of the floor framing so that equal changes in height occur as the beams shrink.

The solution to the problem illustrated in figure 22 involves the additional expense of a second beam. A cheaper alternative is shown in figure 23. The joists are butted against the inner face of the support beam and rest on a 75 mm x 35 mm ledger (or light brackets) nailed or bolted near the lower edge of the beam. The shrinkage of the ledger will only be a fraction of that of the main beam and the slight loss of level would be barely noticeable. Incidentally, square notching of the joists can cause serious loss of strength, but the 1 in 3 sloping cut below the notch will obviate this.

Figure 22. Prevention of differential settlement in a floor

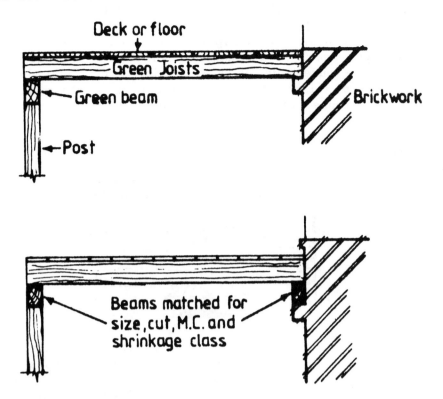

Figure 23. Alternative solution to the problem shown in figure 22

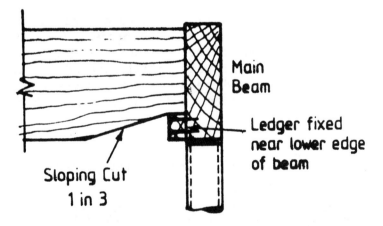

A similar problem is posed by the steel I-beam and wooden joist construction shown in figure 24. Here, the joists rest on ledgers bolted to the web of the I-beam, and the flooring may be laid flush with the top of the steel beam or a packing block may be placed on the top flange to allow the flooring to be nailed down over the beam. As the hardwood joists shrink, the level of the flooring attached to them falls. However, over the steel beam, the flooring cannot move, with the result that marked humps appear in the floor at each beam. There are several ways of avoiding this trouble. In one method, a removable floor section above the steel beam may be adjusted in height by suitable packing strips to correspond with the changing level of the rest of the floor as the timber joists shrink. Another method is shown in figure 25. Here the joists are simply notched out to take a piece of the same green hardwood and this acts as a nailing strip for the floor above it. It is, however, essential that a gap equal to at least 10 per cent of the depth of the joists be left between the underside of the nailing strip and the flange of the I-beam. Then as the joists shrink, the floor as a whole will go down with them without interference from the steel beams.

Figure 24. Shrinkage problems in timber/steel floor systems

In brick veneer construction in housing, the structural frame is often fabricated from green timber and the outer cladding consists of fired-clay bricks to provide protection against the elements and also to impart a pleasant surface with low maintenance. The brickwork remains at a constant height, but the timber frame reduces in height as the green timbers shrink on drying. The total depth of timber subject to shrinkage in the height of the frame amounts to about 300 mm, which may yield a drop in height of from 5 to 40 mm at various positions in the frame. Adequate clearance is required where window-sills, soffit linings and roof rafters project from the frame over the top of brickwork. The provision of the necessary clearance between the soffit and the brickwork near the top of a wall is illustrated in figure 26. Similar precautions must be applied elsewhere to prevent contact between the timber and brick components. In two-storey buildings, the problems become accentuated.

Figure 25. One solution to the problem illustrated in figure 24

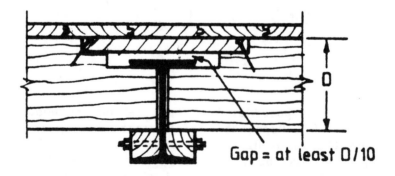

Gap = at least D/10

Figure 26. Provision of clearance between the soffit lining
and brickwork in brick veneer construction

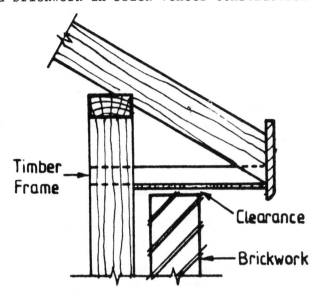

    Metal split-ring connectors and shear plates are used in the joints of
large timber structures to resist high forces. These components are adequa-
tely described in the chapter "Timber connectors" in Strength Characteristics
and Design, the fourth volume in this collection. Precautions must be exer-
cised when installing these fasteners in green timber; otherwise, the timber
in contact with the fasteners can split as it shrinks during drying. The circular groove for split rings must be of the recommended dimensions so that the
gap in the ring will be of the correct clearance, when installed, to allow for
the anticipated shrinkage without offering restraint and causing the timber to
split. When two or more rows of split rings are installed across intersecting
green timber members having different shrinkage characteristics or grain
directions, splitting between the rows can be minimized by making a saw cut
between the rows (figure 27).

Figure 27. Use of a saw cut to reduce end-splitting in green
members subjected to lateral restraint

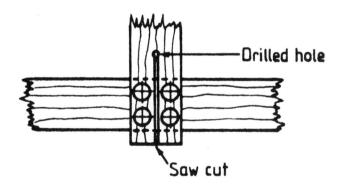

    Shear plates in green timber members can present serious splitting prob-
lems, even with single plates, as the circular plates are of solid material
and do not allow for any adjustment under the lateral forces imposed during

shrinkage of the timber. In such applications the recessed grooves in the timber, which accommodate the shear plates, need to be machined oversize to permit shrinkage free of restraint. The additional slip in the joints, due to clearance in the grooves, needs to be allowed for in design.

The variety of examples described should serve to indicate that the use of green timber need not present serious problems because of shrinkage. Entirely satisfactory structures of all types may be built of this material. It is only necessary to visualize what is going to happen to a structure or to a joint when green timber shrinks and, where necessary, make a simple provision for that shrinkage.

Bibliography

Kauman, W. G. Cell collapse in wood. Holz als Rohund Werkstoff (New York) 22:5:183-196, and 22:12:465-472, 1964.

Kingston, R.S.T. and C.J.E. Risdon. Shrinkageand density of Australian and other South West Pacific woods. Technological paper No. 13. South Melbourne, CSIRO, Division of Forest Products, 1961.

Kloot, N. H. Shrinkage in structural timbers. CSIRO Forest Products Newsletter (South Melbourne) 256, 1959.

Pearson, R. G., Kloot, N. H. and J. D. Boyd. Timber engineering design handbook. Carlton, Victoria, Australia, Melbourne University Press, 1958.

Timber Promotion Committee and Timber Merchants' Association. Technical timber guide. Melbourne, Australia, 1974.

V. POLE STRUCTURES

G. B. Walford*

Introduction

The most common use of poles in developed countries is for the support of overhead transmission lines, although in New Zealand this market has, over the past decade, been eclipsed by a demand for poles for house building. By using poles for the foundations, as in pole platform construction, or as part of the framework as well, as in pole frame construction, previously unusable land has been built on. This fact may be viewed with some amusement by residents of many tropical Pacific nations where for centuries houses have been built on pole foundations to protect against intruders, animals and earthquakes and to improve ventilation. Substantial savings in building costs are obtained by using poles as columns with the butt end embedded in the ground. This application is frequently seen in warehouses. Poles are also used for bridge stringers, shelter fences, retaining walls, wharf piles and lookout tower structures. With a little ingenuity in fabricating joints, poles have been used for beams and rafters in conjunction with pole columns.

Poles have several inherent advantages over sawn timber: they are often the most readily available form of structural timber, particularly in remote areas; the costs and wastage of sawing are eliminated; a pole is always stronger than the laminated beam that can be made from it; and, for reasons to be discussed, higher allowable stresses may be assigned to poles than to sawn timber. Also, trees such as those from plantation thinnings or left as waste in clearfelling operations because they are too small to be utilized economically as sawlogs may be used quite effectively in pole structures, even temporary ones such as the scaffolding seen in many Asian countries.

Poles have two disadvantages: their shape and, for many species, poor durability in ground contact. The development of architectural and constructional techniques for handling the aesthetics and round shape of poles and of a preservation industry that can supply treated pole timbers with a guaranteed life in excess of 80 years even in ground contact has done much to overcome these difficulties. Probably the most outstanding pole frame building in the world is the indigenous performing arts centre at Nairobi, which has a pole frame dome spanning 120 ft (36.6 m).

Useful information on the structural aspects of pole frame buildings is given in the manual of the American Institute of Timber Construction (AITC) [1] and the report by Patterson and Kinney [2]. Guidance on the design of simple pole frame buildings is available from Bournon and Keating [3] and the New Zealand Timber Research and Development Association [4]. Publications on more elaborate pole frame housing have been produced by Degenkolb and others [5], Norton [6] and Blakey [7]. An excellent dossier describing the design and cost of various pole structures has been produced by Lattey [8].

---

*Scientist, Forest Research Institute, Rotorua, New Zealand.

A. Design stresses

The structural characteristics of poles are described in the chapter "Review of timber strength grouping systems" in Structural Timber and Products, the second volume in this collection. The system of assigning stress grades to round timbers adopted in AS 1720 [9] is convenient, and the comparison between these and the stress grades assigned to select grade sawn timber is as shown in table 1.

Table 1. Stress grades for poles and round timbers

| Strength group | Stress grade for green timber | |
	Pole	Select grade sawn
S1	F34	F27
S2	F27	F17
S3	F22	F17
S4	F17	F14
S5	F14	F11
S6	F11	F8/F7
S7	F8	F7

The poles are rated one stress grade higher than the highest grade of sawn timber because the occurrence of natural defects is compensated by the following:

(a) The tension strength of pole timber is increased because the fibres flow smoothly around natural defects and are not terminated as sloping grain at sawn faces;

(b) Many hardwood species have large tension growth stresses around their perimeters, and this assists in increasing the bending strength of the compression face of a pole in bending. The detrimental effect of the growth stresses on the tension face is not important owing to the large tension strength of pole timbers;

(c) In pine species, there is usually an increase in wood density and hence strength properties from the pith to the bark. Thus, the highly stressed wood in a pole in bending is likely to be stronger than the species' average.

The equivalence expressed in table 1 is based on the assumption that poles or logs are from mature trees. If the tree is less than 25 years old when felled or if the pole has fewer than 25 growth rings at the butt end, an adjustment should be made for the effects of immaturity. This effect is shown in the data given in table 2.

A factor predicting a similar effect of maturity on radiata pine poles was deduced from the variation of density with age and its relationship to strength [10] as follows:

	Number of growth rings			
	10	15	20	25
Factor relative to age 15	0.88	1.00	1.09	1.15

Table 2. Effect of age on the strength of green
radiata pine poles

Age of tree (yr)	Modulus of rupture (MPa)
12	39.3
16	38.6
20	46.2
22	43.4
29	52.4
32	52.4

Source: J. D. Boyd, "The strength of Australian pole timbers - IV: radiata pine poles", Technological Paper No. 32 (South Melbourne, CSIRO, Division of Forest Products, 1964).

Another consideration for poles is the effect on strength of bark removal. If the bark is removed manually, e.g. using a spade, machete or draw knife, then it is likely that little damage will be done to the swellings in the trunk around knots. If the bark is removed by machine and the resulting pole has a smooth tapering profile, then some strength will be lost because the natural reinforcement around the knots will have been removed and the sloping grain exposed. The degree of damage depends on the amount of swelling initially. Table 3 gives the losses in modulus of rupture and modulus of elasticity in Corsican pine poles that had an average nodal swelling of 20 mm at each knot whorl and a mean diameter between nodes of 220 mm.

Table 3. Loss in strength and stiffness of poles
due to wood removal from nodal swellings
(Percentage)

Depth of wood removal (mm)	Loss in	
	MOR	MOE
5.75	14	6
15.5	29	15

Source: G. B. Walford, "The effect of mechanical debarking on the strength of Corsican pine poles", New Zealand Forest Service, Forest Research Institute, unpublished FP/TE Report No. 38, 1981.

Since any soil can pick up moisture, the design stresses chosen for embedded poles at the ground-line must always be taken to be those of green timber; for dry poles, e.g. those used in a roof structure, 10-20 per cent higher stresses are reasonable, according to Boyd [11].

B. Design of ground embedment

Poles embedded in the ground may be designed as cantilevers resisting lateral loads. The required depth of embedment may be calculated from appendix K of AS 1720 if the poles are relatively short. For larger poles, the procedure developed by Rutlege is useful and is given in [1] and [2]. This procedure is based on the criterion of a limiting movement of 0.5 in. (12 mm) at ground level on application of design load. Figure 28, reproduced from [2], gives the required depth of embedment for a pole without rigid restraint at the ground-line, e.g. by a concrete floor. It is based on the following formula:

$$D = A[1 + (1 + 2.18 \ H/A)^{0.5}] \qquad (1)$$

where $A = 2.34 \ P/SB$, H is the height above the ground-line at which force P acts, P is the horizontal force acting on the pole, S is the soil pressure at depth 0.34 D below ground level and B is the diameter of the pole, or of the encasing reinforced concrete, or of hard backfill.

If rigid restraint is provided at ground level, the depth of embedment is given by

$$D = (4.25 \ PH/SB)^{0.5} \qquad (2)$$

where S is the allowable lateral soil pressure at depth D below ground level.

The allowable soil pressure S at any specified depth h below the soil surface is the maximum soil passive pressure that can develop. For most soils that are suitable for foundations, a value of S = 12 kPa (250 psf) is conservative. For sand, the passive pressure, in kPa, may be taken from Rankine's formula:

$$S = \frac{1 + \sin \theta}{1 - \sin \theta} \times 19 \ h \qquad (3)$$

where h is in metres and θ is the angle of friction of the sand.

For more general cases, S may be taken to be the lesser of S_1 and S_2 given in table 4.

Table 4. Allowable lateral soil pressure at depth h

Class of material	S_1	S_2 (kPa)
Good: compact, well-graded sand and gravel; hard clay; well-graded fine and coarse sand (all drained so water will not stand)	60 h	380

continued

Table 4 (<u>continued</u>)

Class of material	S_1	S_2 (kPa)
Average: compact fine sand; medium clay; compact sandy loam; loose, coarse sand and gravel (all drained so water will not stand)	30 h	120
Poor: soft clay; clay loam; poorly compacted sand; clays containing large amounts of silt (water stands during wet season)	15 h	70

<u>Source</u>: D. Patterson and E. E. Kinney, <u>Pole Building Design</u> (McLean, Virginia, American Wood Preservers Institute, 1969).

C. Pole connections

Connections are usually the most difficult aspect of the design of pole structures. Some typical details are shown in figure 29, while figures 30 and 31 show less conventional but nevertheless effective connections using steel strapping or threaded steel rods. In the case of the strapping, the same result may be obtained using wire or some form of lashing.

Fasteners used for poles treated with copper-chrome-arsenic (CCA) preservatives can corrode if moisture is present. This problem has been overcome by using (a) stainless steel strapping or bolts etc., (b) galvanized steel bolts protected by plastic tubing or (c) galvanized steel bolts and hardware liberrally coated in grease.

D. Examples

Figure 32 gives schematic diagrams of various structures described in detail in [3], [5] and [8]:

(a) A simple monopitch frame that relies on the embedment of the poles for its resistance to lateral loads;

(b) A tied eaves portal design that reduces the reliance on cantilever action of the pole columns. Steel rod or wire makes a satisfactory tie. It needs provision for tightening, e.g. a turnbuckle in the rod or a Spanish windlass in the wire;

(c) A two-bay unbraced or tied portal that can be extended to as many bays as desired. This design can be used to produce a round structure with a single central pole;

(d) Trusses on poles, which is a common design for haybarns in New Zealand;

(e) Pole platform construction, a quick method, provides a level support for conventional light frame construction;

(f) Pole frame construction, which results when the poles are carried through to support the roof and/or the building is on several levels down a slope;

(g) A simple scissor truss that can be made using slender poles and bolts.

Figure 28.   Chart for embedment of posts with overturning loads

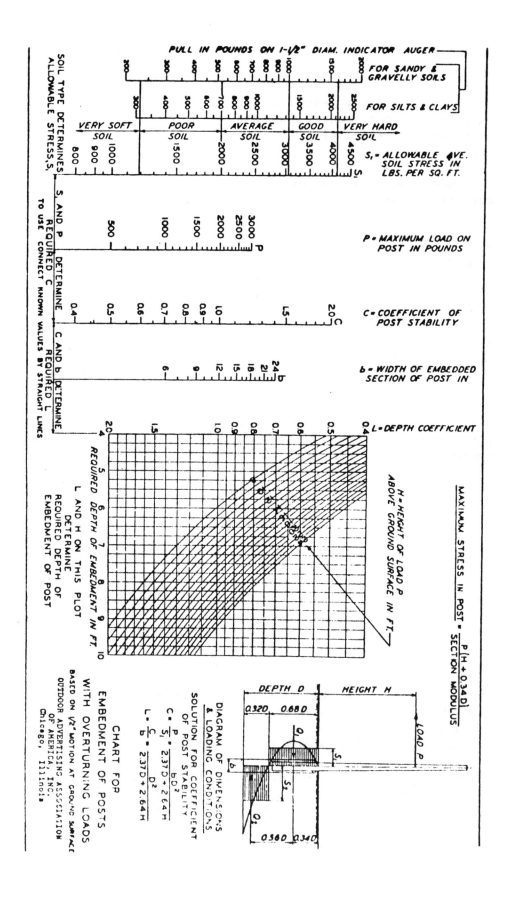

- 35 -

Figure 29. Detail of typical pole connection

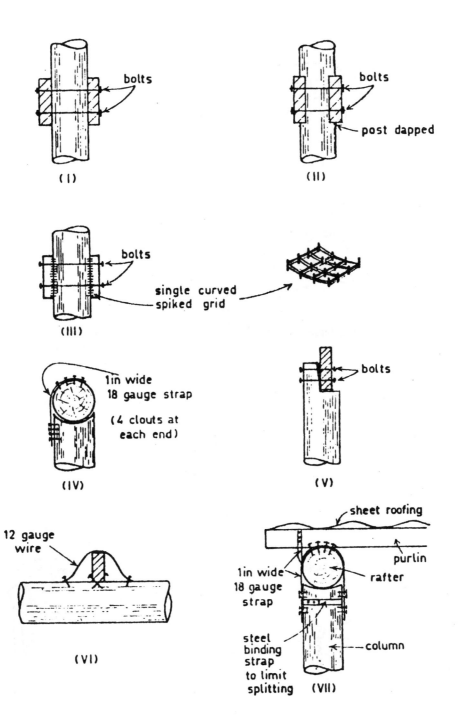

Figure 30.   Connections using steel strapping

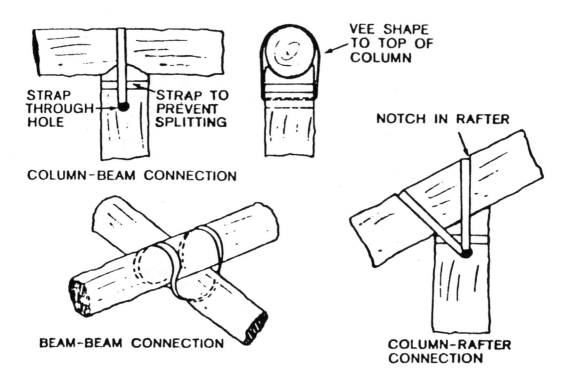

Figure 31.   Connections using threaded steel rod

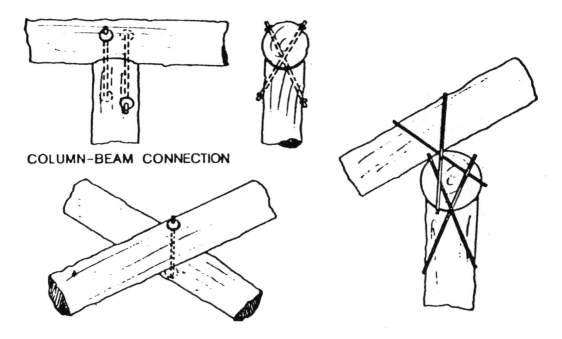

Figure 32.   Examples of pole structures

A.   Simple monopitch frame

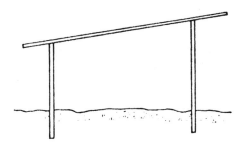

B.   Tied eaves portal frame

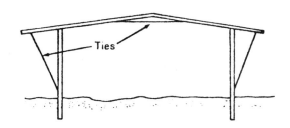

C.   Two-bay unbraced or
     tied portal frame

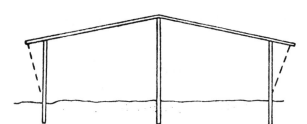

D.   Poles supporting trusses

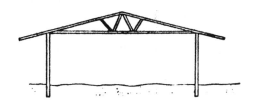

E.   Pole platform

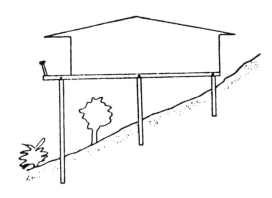

F.   Pole frame

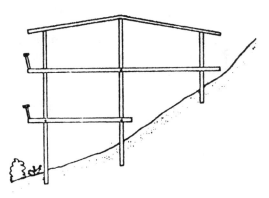

G.   W Truss made from poles and bolts

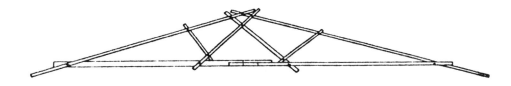

References

1. American Institute of Timber Construction, <u>Timber Construction Manual</u> (New York, John Wiley, 1966), pp. 4.83-4.93.

2. D. Patterson and E. E. Kinney, <u>Pole Building Design</u> (McLean, Virginia, American Wood Preservers Institute, 1969).

3. R. N. Bournon and W. G. Keating, "Designs for pole frame buildings", Technical Note No. 7 (South Melbourne, CSIRO, Division of Forest Products, 1971).

4. "Pole frame buildings", <u>New Zealand Timber Research and Development Association: Timber and Wood Products Manual</u>, Section 2b-1 (Wellington, 1972).

5. H. Degenkolb and others, <u>Federal Housing Authority: Pole House Construction</u> (McLean, Virginia, American Wood Preservers Institute, 1975).

6. P. Norton, <u>The New Zealand Pole House</u> (Hicksons Timber Impregnation Co., 1976).

7. J. Blakey, "Pole type construction", <u>New Zealand Timber Research and Development Association: Timber and Wood Products Manual</u>, Section 2f-1 (Wellington, 1973).

8. P. Lattey, <u>Pole Buildings in Papua New Guinea</u> (Boroko, Papua New Guinea, Forest Products Centre, 1974).

9. Standards Association of Australia, <u>Australian Standard 1720-1975: SAA Timber Engineering Code</u> (Sydney, 1975).

10. G. B. Walford, "Design criteria and specification of poles", <u>Seminar on Roundwood Products of the Future</u> (Wellington, New Zealand Timber Research and Development Association, 1975).

11. J. D. Boyd, "The strength of Australian pole timbers - IV: radiata pine poles", Technological Paper No. 32 (South Melbourne, CSIRO, Division of Forest Products, 1964).

VI. TIMBER FRAMING FOR HOUSING

Bernie T. Hawkins*

Introduction

In Australia, about 80 per cent of housing is constructed with a basic frame, usually of timber, lined internally with some sort of plaster board and clad externally, most often with a veneer of bricks. About 15 per cent is clad externally with timber boards or cement sheet boards.

House framing represents by far the largest use of structural timber in Australia. AS 1684-1979, Timber Framing Code [1], and its predecessors, have been used for many years to ensure that safe, satisfactory houses and other buildings are erected in the most economical manner possible.

In this chapter, the Code is looked at in detail, and other factors involved in the building and performance of house frames are considered.

The terminology for framing members is illustrated in figure 33.

A. History of the Code

In 1941 the first edition of Pamphlet 112 of the CSIRO Division of Forest Products appeared. Entitled "Building frames - timber and sizes", the pamphlet was very simple and offered only a very few variations for spacing, loadings etc. Nevertheless, because at that time there was little variation in the types of house being built, it was in great demand by architects, builders, specifiers etc. A revised and expanded edition was brought out in 1952, but by the late 1960s the changes in strength groupings and stress grades, together with an increase in the variety of houses being built, necessitated a more comprehensive document. This document was CA 38, the Light Timber Framing Code, first published by the Standards Association of Australia in 1971. Since that time, the Code has been metricated and revised on four occasions, until today it is AS 1684-1979, Timber Framing Code. As an Australian standard, this Code was written under the direction of a committee comprising mainly builders, timber suppliers, wood technologists and representatives of timber and building associations and specifiers.

B. Content of the Code

The Code is a 56-page document divided into six sections:

Section 1, Scope and General
Section 2, Substructure
Section 3, Timber Floor Framing and Flooring
Section 4, Timber Wall Framing
Section 5, Timber Roof Framing
Section 6, Nailing and Anchorage

---

*An officer of CSIRO, Division of Building Research, Melbourne.

Figure 33.   Nomenclature for framing members

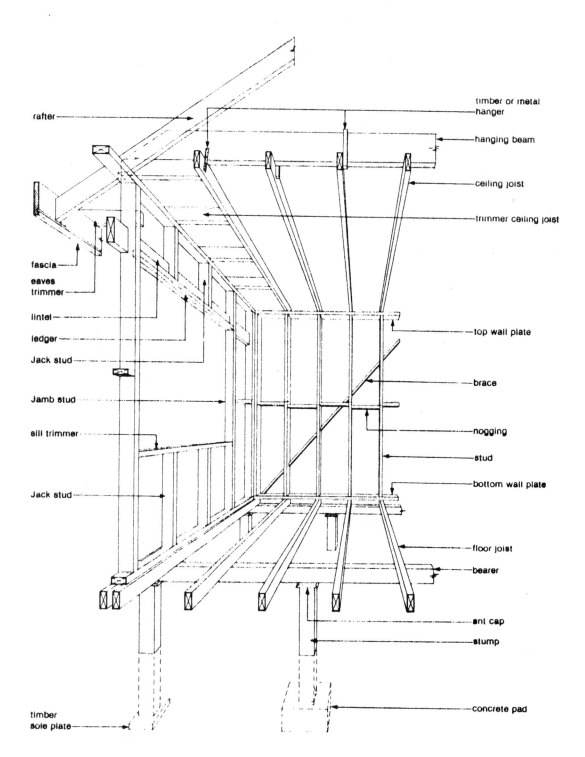

It contains four appendices dealing with the properties and grades of structural timber, site preparation, storage and handling of timber and precaution against wind effects.

In section 1, as might be expected, terms are defined, general rules are given for such matters as interpolation between values in the tables and other information is given on the use of the tables. In addition, advice is given on the storage and handling of timber.

Section 2 gives details of site preparation and the foundation necessary for frame construction. It also gives information on such matters as sub-floor ventilation and termite protection.

Sections 4, 5 and 6 deal with the selection and placement of the various members throughout the frame. Details are given on bracing requirements (both temporary and permanent), drilling and notching of members etc., and other aspects of workmanship. This is a very important part of the Code and will be discussed further.

Section 6 gives the number and diameter of nails used in various parts of the frame. It also discusses alternative methods of fixing.

Several other parts of the Code have been issued as supplements. Each supplement concentrates on timber of one stress grade and one moisture class, giving the details of the spans etc. that can be supported by various sizes of timber under various spacings etc. Each supplement contains 33 tables, 15(A)-27S, covering the members shown in table 5.

Table 5. Members covered by the tables in timber framing code supplements

Table No.	Member
1S(A)	Bearers supporting single-storey load-bearing walls: maximum spacing of bearers parallel to wall, 1.8 m
1S(B)	Bearers supporting single-storey load-bearing walls: maximum spacing of bearers parallel to wall, 3.6 m
2S	Bearers supporting floor joists only
3S	Floor joists
4S(A)	Studs for single-storey load-bearing walls: studs spaced up to 450 mm apart
4S(B)	Studs for single-storey load-bearing walls: studs spaced up to 600 mm apart
5S	Studs supporting concentration of loading
6S	Studs at sides of openings: single-storey constructions or upper storey of two-storey constructions

continued

Table 5 (<u>continued</u>)

Table No.	Member
7S	Top wall plates: single or upper storey
8S	Bottom wall plates: single or upper storey
9S	Lintels: single or upper storey
10S	Ceiling joists supporting ceiling only
11S	Hanging beams for ceiling joists
12S	Ceiling battens
13S(A)	Rafters or roofing purlins: supported at two points only
13S(B)	Rafters or roofing purlins: continuous over two or more spans
14S	Roof beams (principals) for non-trafficable roofs
15S	Strutting beams for roof members
16S	Underpurlins
17S	Roofing battens
18S	Verandah posts
19S(A)	Bearers supporting two-storey load-bearing walls: maximum spacing of bearers parallel to wall, 1.8 m
19S(B)	Bearers supporting two-storey load-bearing walls: maximum spacing of bearers parallel to wall, 3.6 m
20S	Bearers cantilevered to support balconies
21S	Joists for upper floors and permissible cantilever to support balconies
22S(A)	Studs for upper storey load-bearing walls: studs spaced up to 450 mm apart
22S(B)	Studs for upper storey load-bearing walls: studs spaced up to 600 mm apart
23S(A)	Studs for lower storey load-bearing walls: studs spaced up to 450 mm apart
23S(B)	Studs for lower storey load-bearing walls: studs spaced up to 600 mm apart
24S	Studs at sides of openings in lower storey load-bearing walls

continued

Table 5 (<u>continued</u>)

Table No.	Member
25S	Top wall plates for lower storey load-bearing walls
26S	Bottom wall plates for lower storey load-bearing walls
27S	Lintels in lower storey load-bearing walls

There are 22 supplements at present, whose coverage ranges from unseasoned timber of F4 grade to seasoned hardwood of F27 grade. The titles of the various supplements are shown in table 6.

Table 6. List of supplements containing light
timber framing span tables

Supplement No.	Description of timber
1	Unseasoned timber, stress grade F4
2	Unseasoned timber, stress grade F5
3	Unseasoned timber, stress grade F7
4	Unseasoned timber, stress grade F8
5	Unseasoned timber, stress grade F11
6	Unseasoned timber, stress grade F14
7	Unseasoned timber, stress grade F17
8	Unseasoned timber, stress grade F22
9	Seasoned softwood, stress grade F5
10	Seasoned softwood, stress grade F7
11	Seasoned softwood, stress grade F8
12	Seasoned softwood, stress grade F11
13	Seasoned hardwood, stress grade F11
14	Seasoned hardwood, stress grade F14
15	Seasoned hardwood, stress grade F17
16	Seasoned hardwood, stress grade F27
17	Unseasoned timber (alternative sizes), stress grade F4
18	Unseasoned timber (alternative sizes), stress grade F5
19	Unseasoned timber (alternative sizes), stress grade F8
20	Unseasoned timber (alternative sizes), stress grade F11
21	Seasoned softwood, stress grade F4
22	Seasoned softwood, stress grade F14

C. Use of the Code

To establish member sizes and/or spans for the various parts of a framed structure, it is first necessary to refer to the appropriate section of the main Code. For example, to find a suitable ceiling joist to span 2.4 m in dry radiata pine of F5 stress grade, section 5.2.2 would be referred to. Here, amongst information on spacing, direction, splicing and method of support, it is learned that table 10S is the table in the appropriate supplement that will give the size of material necessary to span 2.4 m. However, when table 10S in supplement No. 9, which is for F5 seasoned softwood is consulted, it can be seen that the spacing of the joists must first be decided. If the joists are to be supported at two points only, then the table shows that if the spacing is 600 mm it is necessary to use a 120 x 35 joist. This table also shows, however, that if it is desired to put a hanging beam halfway across the span, 70 x 45 joists could be used, because these are capable of spanning 1.4 m, and in this case it is desired only to span 1/2 of 2.4 m.

It is possible, of course, to start with a given timber size and use a table to find the maximum span it can carry.

Some members, particularly wall members, are not as easily defined because their size etc. are determined mainly by the amount of roof load they have to carry. Consequently it became necessary to introduce a variable that defines the amount of roof load carried by a wall member. This variable is called effective roof length, or EL, and is defined in figure 7 of the Code. It must be stressed that although that figure shows roofing members, it has nothing to do with the actual roof itself but is merely a means of defining how much load goes onto the wall members from the roof. An estimate of the load on an external wall due to the roof weight is obtained by multiplying (unit width of wall) x (half of EL plus length of eaves overhang) x (mass of roof per unit area).

Overall, it can be seen that the tables in the Code offer a wide range of options for the designer and/or builder in sizes, spans and stress grades, and that the main body of the Code sets a standard for workmanship that must be met if the tables are to be used efficiently.

D. Technical basis of the Code

A reasonably detailed description of the technical matters involved in producing the tables in the Code is contained in Low-Rise Domestic and Similar Framed Structures - Part 1, which is published by CSIRO, Division of Building Research. Some of the main factors involved are as follows:

(a) Dead loads are calculated from the masses of various building materials given in AS 1170, SAA Loading Code, Part I [2]. However, some modifications are made to the self-weight factor to allow for the higher stress grades usually coming from denser species;

(b) Live loads are those specified by AS 1170 for various parts of the structure;

(c) The wind loading adopted for calculations in AS 1684 is that due to an effective wind velocity of 33 m/sec. The effective wind velocity is obtained by establishing the regional basic wind velocity for a given return period and multiplying it by a factor known as the terrain category factor, which depends on the height of the structure and the nature of the surroundings. For the built-up metropolitan area of Brisbane, the relevant figures are 50 m/sec for a regional basic wind velocity with a 50-year-return period and a multiplying factor of 0.65 for a terrain category 3, up to 5 m height of building. This represents the upper limit of 33 m/sec used in the Code;

(d) The chapter "Derivation of design properties" in <u>Strength Characteristics and Design</u>, the fourth volume in this collection, explains how the basic working stresses are derived for each stress grade from the known strength properties of the timber. However, before these allowable stresses are used, they can be modified to suit the particular situation in which the timber is to be used. The modification factors are all discussed in AS 1720 [3]. Some of the more important ones occurring in AS 1684 are as follows:

(i)   Duration of load. Many of the loads dealt with in the Code are of short duration, e.g. a man carrying a heavy weight or a local, dense crowd. In these cases, the working stress may be 56 per cent higher than for permanent loads. In the case of the shortest load, i.e. a wind load, the working stress is allowed to be doubled; in calculating member deflections under dead loads, the short-term deformation must be multiplied by a factor of 3 in the case of initially green timber or 2 in the case of seasoned timber;

(ii) Moisture content. Most framing timbers used in a green or partly dry condition are of a size such that the timber dries to equilibrium moisture content within a year. Tests have shown that hardwood species in Australia generally increase in load-carrying capacity by about 25 per cent on drying, despite the reduction in size due to shrinkage. To take this into account, the working stresses have been increased by 15 per cent for members up to 38 mm thick, by 10 per cent for members 50 mm thick and by 5 per cent for members 75 mm thick. Above this thickness it is considered that drying would be too slow for any adjustment to be made to working stresses;

(iii) Temperature. Variations in ambient temperatures throughout most of Australia are usually accompanied by a compensating variation in the moisture content of the timber. For this reason, although timber gets weaker with increasing temperature, it is only in the northern coastal regions, where high temperatures coincide with high humidities, that it is necessary to take some action. In that case, the basic working stresses are reduced by 10 per cent;

(iv) Load sharing. Where a group of members act together as a system, two factors operate to assist the system. Firstly, if one member of the group is weaker than the others and reaches its ultimate load-carrying capacity, the system may continue to sustain an increasing load because the adjacent members are stiffer and stronger. Allowance is made for this effect by allowing an increase of 15 per cent in working stresses for members spaced at 450 mm, diminishing to no increase for members spaced 1,200 mm or more apart. Secondly, where members of a system cannot deflect independently of other members, such as in a two or three-layer grid system, localized loads are distributed laterally to more members than those directly under the load. The effective concentrated load that must be considered in these cases is given in Rule 3.2.7 of AS 1720;

(e) The minimum dimensions of timber allowed when the spans specified in the Code are used are shown in each table in the supplements. In general, green timber can be 3 or 4 mm less than the size nominated, but dry timber cannot be less;

(f) Design criteria. Virtually all the members of a framed structure, with the obvious exception of members such as stumps and struts, act as beams, with wall studs being treated as beam-columns. The maximum allowable span is determined as the minimum value of the following:

(i) Maximum span of adequate bending strength under dead loads alone, including the self-weight of the member, and under the combined dead and live loads;

(ii) Maximum span of adequate shear strength under the same loading conditions;

(iii) Maximum span with acceptable long-term deflection under live loads;

For roof members:

(iv) Maximum span of adequate bending strength under combined dead and wind loads;

For wall members:

(v) Also maximum span of adequate bending strength under the combined vertically applied dead and wind loads, together with the transversely applied wind load.

The tables in Low-Rise Domestic and Similar Framed Structures - Part I give full details on all these criteria. Table 7 below summarizes deflection criteria for the major members in a house frame.

Table 7. Deflection criteria

Member	Maximum permissible deflection	
	Dead load only	Live load only
Members subjected to foot traffic	span/300, max. 12 mm	span/360, max. 9 mm
Rafters and purlins	span/300, max. 20 mm	span/300, max. 12 mm
Ceiling joists and hangers	span/300, max. 12 mm	span/270, max. 15 mm
Strutting beams, supporting rafters and ceiling joists	span/300, max. 12 mm	span/300, max. 12 mm

continued

Table 7 (<u>continued</u>

Member	Maximum permissible deflection	
	Dead load only	Live load only
Wall plates	span/240, max. 6 mm	span/240, max. 6 mm
Lintels	span/300, max. 9 mm	span/240, max. 9 mm
Studs	span/300, max. 9 mm	span/360, max. 9 mm (live roof load) span/240, max. 12 mm (wind load)

E. Future of the Code

The Code is being continuously reviewed by a committee of the Standards Association of Australia and is revised every few years. Extra material is periodically disseminated by bodies such as CSIRO.

F. Workmanship

AS 1684 assumes that the workmanship is of such a standard that all members are capable of resisting the forces assumed in the engineering calculations used to develop the span tables etc. In general, the standard of work of carpenters involved in house framing is reasonable; however, there are occasional difficulties, particularly where later trades modify structural members. It is usually up to the building inspector to detect gross departures from good building practice or good quality workmanship. The following examples are taken from a series of articles by N. H. Kloot that appeared in Forest Products Newsletter No. 400, 1975, which used to be published by CSIRO, Division of Building Research. It should be pointed out that, in the cases described, the building inspector had not yet inspected the building and would have demanded that the faults be corrected as soon as he had detected them.

1. The Barap tie

The so-called Barap tie is now commonly employed as an effective means of increasing the strength and stiffness of a timber member such as a hip rafter when used over a rather large span. This tie is basically a steel rod fastened to each end of the timber member and propped away from it with a strut (figure 34). The principle on which the Barap tie operates is by no means new and is well known to engineers as the king or queen post truss. When the truss is under load, the tie is stressed in tension and the whole structural unit becomes equivalent to a beam much deeper than the actual timber member used.

Figure 34. Use of the Barap tie to stiffen and strengthen a hip rafter;
trussed beam with king post (top) and with queen post (below)

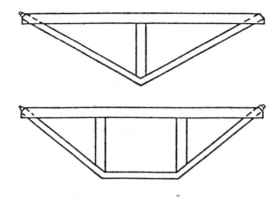

Figure 35 illustrates a Barap tie fitted to a hip rafter, the strut being
comprised of two small timber offcuts bearing on two underpurlins which, in
turn, are nailed to the hip rafter. For practical purposes, the tie, as
applied in this case, is useless. Between the steel rod and the hip rafter
there is approximately 200 mm of side-grain green timber. Even allowing a
conservative 5 per cent for shrinkage, the intended strut will shrink 10 mm.
This will have the effect of completely unloading the steel tie so that the
hip rafter itself will have to carry the full load. Obviously it is too small
to do this, for otherwise a Barap tie would not have been fitted in the first
place. Thus, the rafter will eventually sag well beyond the limits allowed
for this type of member.

Figure 35. Green timber used on its edge as a prop for a Barap tie
means that the tie becomes useless as the timber shrinks

Figure 36 shows another such installation, only in this instance a steel
prop has been used.

Unfortunately, this prop is bearing on the side grain of a packing piece,
which, in turn, is bearing on two underpurlins. Here again, shrinkage will
tend to unload the steel tie, although not to quite the same extent as in the
previous example.

Figure 36. The steel prop goes part of the way towards making the
Barap tie effective. Shrinkage of the packing piece, however,
will tend to reduce the tie's effectiveness

For a Barap tie to be fully effective, the strut should be of steel, as
in figure 36, or should be a piece of timber loaded on end grain. Moreover,
the top end of the strut should bear directly onto the timber member to which
the tie has been fitted.

2. Notching for braces

A stud, particularly in the outer wall, has to carry its share of the
roof weight as well as resist horizontal wind forces even when the structure
is clad with brick veneer. Yet in spite of its importance, the stud is
probably the most abused of all of the structural members.

Notches decrease the strength of studs and to some degree their stiffness, the decrease being greatest when the notch is near the centre of the
height of the stud. In preparing the tables for notched studs in AS 1684, an
allowance was made for loss of strength in a stud when the notch was no more
than 5 mm deeper than the specified thickness of the brace.

Figure 37 shows a notch cut into a pine stud to a depth nearly twice the
thickness of the brace. Furthermore, it can be seen that the stud has
actually broken at a knot cluster immediately at the back of the notch. As a
load-carrying member, this stud will be totally ineffective. The performance
of the stud shown in figure 38 would be well below that for which it has been
designed after the plumber has made himself a notch immediately behind that
carrying the timber brace.

Figure 37. General notch in a stud. Note also failure of the stud
at the knot cluster

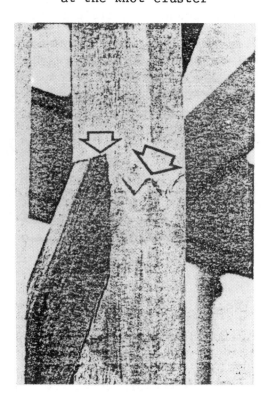

Figure 38. A notch like this might suit a plumber, but the stud's
effectiveness as a roof support is almost negligible

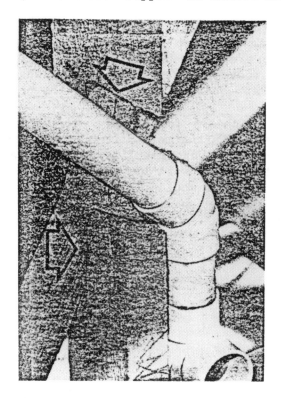

In figure 39, the notch is longer than necessary and, although not clearly defined in the photograph, the initial sawcuts made to allow the timber to be removed for the notch are substantially deeper than required. A similar example of bad workmanship is illustrated in figure 40.

Figure 39. This stud's strength and stiffness have been seriously reduced by excessive and unnecessary notching

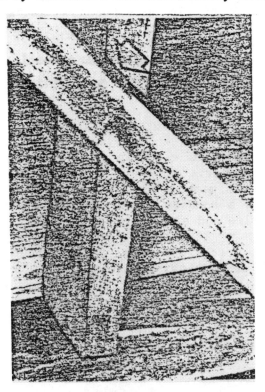

Figure 40. Another example of bad notching

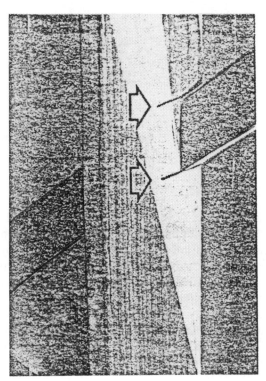

If the overcutting or overnotching occurred once or twice by accident in a whole house frame, the overall effect would not be serious. However, it usually happens that if one stud is overcut or overnotched, practically all the studs are similarly abused. This is a clear case of bad workmanship.

Even if a frame is constructed in accordance with Pamphlet No. 112, mentioned at the beginning of this chapter, poor workmanship later on could be critical. While the pamphlet recommends larger sizes for some members than those allowed in AS 1684, this is no safeguard against poor workmanship. In fact, the larger sizes may give the ill-informed builder a false sense of security when he starts to cut notches, drill holes etc. in studs and other members. It is of interest that whereas the pamphlet has no provisions for controlling the quality of the workmanship, AS 1684 has such provisions, including allowable depths of notches and sizes of drilled holes.

3. Overcutting

The advent of the portable electric saw has certainly made the job much easier for the on-site framer. At the same time, the overcutting of notches in studs, props and other members appears far more prevalent than it once was. The tradesman with a handsaw was unlikely to overcut, except in error, because this took more time and extra physical effort.

Figure 41 shows the notch in a ridge prop overcut badly both horizontally and vertically. As the prop dries, splitting from the end of the vertical cut is likely, in which case the prop will probably become largely ineffective.

Figure 41. Excessive overcutting of notch in a ridge prop

Figure 42 adds to the examples already given of the gross overnotching of studs.

4. Making do

Very frequently at a building site a large pile of timber off-cuts accumulates, and it is only reasonable that as much as possible of this off-cut material is put to sound, practical use. However, improper use of this material on the basis of "making do" or "near enough is good enough", as illustrated in figure 43, is definitely unsound building practice; figure 44 shows an even worse example. Noggings, particularly those at mid-height of the studs, serve an important structural function and are not there just to provide fixing for the wall linings. They also provide restraint against buckling of the studs in the plane of the wall. The noggings illustrated in figures 43 and 44 cannot possibly perform this duty.

- 53 -

Figure 42. Another example of overnotching of stud and top plate

Figure 43. This stud does not get much help from the noggings

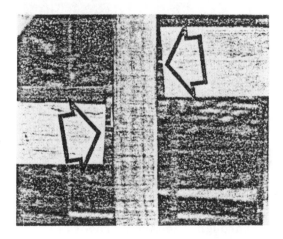

Figure 44. Another ineffectual nogging

Figure 45 shows another example of making do. Here the two pieces of top plate have been joined with a piece of galvanized iron plate. Such a joint, particularly with the nailing use, i.e. one nail on one side, two on the other, serves no useful purpose. Indeed it has not even helped to keep the plates in the same line.

Figure 45. The galvanized plate linking the pieces of top plate is no more than a token gesture; it is difficult to imagine it performing any useful function

A case of near enough being not good enough is shown in figure 46. The header has been cut too short; it is virtually hanging on the nails at its ends instead of sitting on the base of the notches cut in the studs to receive it. Any roof load that happens to fall on the top plate would probably be transferred to the ground through the architraves.

Figure 46. The header is more of a hanging beam, hanging on the nails

5. Props

Figure 47 shows an underpurlin prop at an angle of 70° to the vertical. At this angle it cannot do its job effectively. The builder seems to have had second thoughts, because the end of the underpurlin has been packed up with mortar from the brickwork. When the mortar has set, it will probably be much more effective than the timber prop.

Figure 47. The mortar is doing more to support this underpurlin than the carefully notched strut

6. Party walls

The type of unit construction illustrated in figure 48 is becoming increasingly common. Building regulations require a brick party wall between the units. The builder of these units has made sure not only that the units were divided according to regulations but also that they were seen to be divided. Because no allowance, or only a totally inadequate allowance, has been made for the roof members (whether rafters or trusses) to sag, as they inevitably will do, the roof battens are now bearing on the party walls. The consequent effect, which is accentuated by the long length of unbroken roof, is hardly pleasing to the eye. A similar effect results when an extra rafter is placed each side of the party wall, as in figure 49. These extra rafters, at much closer centres than the common rafters, make the roof much stiffer at the party wall because each of the rafters is more lightly loaded than the rest. They will therefore not sag as much, and the roof will show a wave over the top of the party wall. A uniform spacing of all the rafters would avoid this problem.

Figure 48. The appearance of these units has been spoilt
because insufficient clearance was provided between the
party walls and the roof system

Figure 49. A wave in the roofline can be expected over the party wall
because of the greater rigidity of the doubled-up rafters in this area

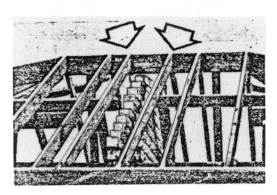

Most of the sag in the roof members takes place in the first 12 months
after the tiles have been laid. So in these examples, which are typical of
many that can be seen around Melbourne, the overall fresh and clean appearance
of new buildings has been quickly depreciated by the poor appearance of the
roofline.

G. Thermal considerations

Since the thermal requirements of a building vary considerably for different climates, the thermal performance of any particular type of construction
may be satisfactory in one location and completely unsatisfactory in another.

A study by Walsh, Gurr and Ballantyne [4] describes the performance of
various types of dwellings in a wide range of climates. It appears that the
use of insulating material is of more significance than whether a wall is of
cavity brick construction or brick veneer.

H. Acoustic considerations

In general, the acoustic performance of a domestic structure is determined by the number of doors, windows etc. However, appendix A of AS 2021 [5] gives acoustic performance information for several different types of construction. Other information is available in a technical study of the Australian Experimental Building Station [6].

I. Cost of construction

On-site costs account for about 75 per cent of the selling price of moderate-sized Australian houses. Of this amount, about two thirds is for materials and one third is for labour. About 60 per cent of the on-site cost is spent on the actual structure of the house.

Several self-explanatory tables from a paper by Woodhead on the producvity of various methods of building different parts of a frame [7], are reproduced here as tables 8-16.

Table 8. Distribution of housing construction cost
(Percentage)

| Item | Share of cost | |
	Individual	Total
Foundations and floor	10–15	
Walls	25–30	60
Roof	18–23	
Fixings, finishes and extras	~ 25	40
Services	~ 15	

- 58 -

Table 9. Distribution of on-site time for elements of
the house construction process
(Percentage)

Element	Brick veneer house on timber subfloor, "economy" quality finishes	Cavity brick house on concrete slab, "medium" quality finishes
Subfloor and floor	13	7
Walls	24	29
Roof	<u>13</u>	<u>16</u>
Total	50	52
Services		
Plumbing	10	5
Electrical	<u>2</u>	<u>3</u>
Total	12	8
Finishes		
Timber	17	10
Paint	14	13
Tiles etc.	<u>2</u>	<u>9</u>
Total	33	32
Extras: concreting, fence and cleaning	5	8

Table 10. Productivity of site preparation for domestic
structures with concrete slabs

Site type	Productivity (man-hrs/100m^2)
Flat slope < 1:25	3-6
Medium slope 1:25 to 1:10	6-12
Difficult sloping sites, substantial cut and fill, perhaps rock	12-30+

Table 11. Productivity of construction for domestic
structures with concrete slabs

Slab type	Productivity (man-hrs/100m^2)
Light raft	40-55
Light or medium raft with internal beams	55-80
Suspended raft	80+

Table 12. Productivity for concrete slabs and
conventional subfloors at ground level

Site conditions	Productivity (man-hrs/100m^2)	
	Concrete slab	Conventional subfloor
Easy	40-60	60-70
Less easy	60-90	70-80
Difficult	90-130+	80-100

Table 13. Productivity for laying timber strip and sheet floors

Location	Type of house and floor	Flooring	Productivity (man-hrs/100m^2)
Victoria	Ground level, laid room by room	4" hardwood	16
Queensland	Platform, part ground level	3" hardwood	18
Queensland	High set, platform	Plywood	16
Victoria	Ground level, platform	Plywood	10
Victoria	Ground level, platform	Plywood	8

Table 14. Productivity for wall frame construction

Location	Type	Number of sites	Productivity (man-hrs/100 lineal metres)		
			Factory c/	Site	Total
Victoria	Site-cut softwood	1	Not applicable	47	47
Victoria	Site-cut hardwood	3	Not applicable	40, 50, 52	40–52
Queensland	Site-cut hardwood (elevated house)	1	Not applicable	84	84
New South Wales	Pre-cut timbers, hardwood	2	22	23, 27	45–49
Queensland	Pre-cut timbers, softwood	1	Not available	40	–
Australian Capital Territory	Pre-assembled frame, softwood	1	24	24	48
Victoria	System with mainly steel studs, timber plates and noggings a/	3	Not applicable	23, 23, 24	23
Victoria	System welded steel b/ and timber top plate	3	26–35	9, 12, 14	35–49

a/ Steel studs delivered to site complete with clips for fixing; timber dressed but not cut to length.

b/ Rolled steel channel delivered to factory in set lengths.

c/ Factory time does not include handling.

Table 15. Productivity and distribution of time for the
sub-elements of 12 roofs (excluding ceilings)

Sub-element	Average productivity (man-hrs/100 m^2) covered area)	Share of total roof time (%)
Roof frame	19	29
Fascia	4	6
Plumbing (exluding downpipes)	5	8
Battens and tiles	18	27
Eaves (frame and lining)	10	15
Gables (frame and trim)	<u>10</u>	<u>15</u>
Total	66	100

Table 16. Productivity levels for 12 roof frames (excluding the frame for the gable end, where applicable)

Location	Method of construction	Roof type a/	Area to fascia (m²)	Productivity (man-hrs/100 m² covered area)
Victoria	Site-cut hardwood	3 hips	147	18
Victoria	Site-cut hardwood	3 hips	165	23
Victoria	Site-cut hardwood	3 hips	165	29
Queensland	Site-cut hardwood (house raised 6 ft off the ground)	3 gambrel gables	177	25
			Average:	24
Australian Capital Territory	Trusses b/	2 plain gables	129	8
South Australia	Trusses b/, c/	2 plain gables	130	15
Victoria	Trusses and intermediate joists	2 plain gables	164	23
Western Australia	Trusses and site-cut pieces d/	L-shaped, 2 gambrel gables	240	10
Queensland	Trusses and ceiling battens (high set house)	2 plain gables	101	31 e/
			Average:	14
New South Wales	Pre-cut hardwood timbers	Hips	121	12
New South Wales	Pre-cut hardwood timbers	Hips	103	11
Queensland	Pre-cut softwood timbers	2 hips	174	22
			Average:	15

a/ All roofs designed for tiles except for the Queensland house with 2 plain gables, which was clad with corrugated iron; fascia not included.

b/ Time for installation of ceiling battens estimated at 6 man-hrs.

c/ Fixed by complex brackets.

d/ Ceiling battens took 38 per cent of the time.

e/ This was an atypical roof constructed by day labour and was not included in the average.

References

1. Standards Association of Australia, <u>Australian Standard 1684-1979: SAA Timber Framing Code</u> (Sydney, 1979).

2. Standards Association of Australia, <u>Australian Standard 1170: SAA Loading Code, Part 1 - Dead and Live Loads</u> (Sydney, 1979) and <u>Part 2 - Wind Forces</u> (Sydney, 1980).

3. Standards Association of Australia, <u>Australian Standard 1720: SAA Timber Engineering Code</u> (Sydney, 1975).

4. P. F. Walsh, I. A. Gurr and E. R. Ballantyne, "A comparison of thermal performance of heavyweight and lightweight construction in Australian dwellings", Technical Paper (Second Series) No. 44 (Melbourne, CSIRO, Division of Building Research).

5. Standards Association of Australia, <u>Australian Standard 2021: Code of Practice for Building Siting and Construction against Aircraft Noise Intrusion</u> (Sydney).

6. E. J. Weston, M. A. Burgess and J. A. Whitlock, "Airborne sound transmission through elements of buildings", Technical Study 48, Australian Experimental Building Station.

7. W. D. Woodhead, "Achievable improvements in house building productivity", Paper presented at the Twelfth National Convention of the Housing Industry Association (South Melbourne, April 1977).

VII. CASE STUDY OF TIMBER CONSTRUCTION: KENYA HOTEL

Peter A. Campbell*

Introduction

This case study is based on works carried out on a 200-bed tourist hotel on the Kenya coast and completed in 1974. At the time, the writer was a consulting engineer and was responsible for all timber, reinforced concrete and steel structural works on the site. The purpose of the study is to describe some of the problems that arose with the use of timber and some of the solutions that were found.

The client was a German tourist organization that wanted the hotel to have a strong architectural character. This was something that the architects and the writer had been able to achieve in several hotels, partly by using more timber than was normally used in Kenya.

A. Technical background

The hotel was to be built on top of a low cliff a few metres from the sea and so would be exposed to sea breezes throughout the year. The equilibrium moisture content (emc) was 16-18 per cent, damp enough for the so-called dry-wood termites, Cryptomeres spp., which were very active all along the coast. Subterranean termites were also present as the soils were predominantly sandy, and in the prevailing moist conditions, they were active throughout the year. The margins against decay were low, and any minor leaks would dry out slowly and encourage decay. However, the salt in the air would to some extent counter this threat. Moreover, the salt and the ambient temperature of around 30° C made the problem of rust a very significant consideration in the design of both the steel work and the reinforced concrete and served to stimulate the use of timber.

The general construction was to be of reinforced concrete with walling of exposed, site-cut coral blocks. The roof over the whole hotel complex was of palm thatch on mangrove poles, following traditional construction methods. Under this in the bedrooms and kitchen were concrete slabs (for fire reasons). Elsewhere, over the larger spans, a combination of timber and concrete beams supported the roofs. The general construction was limited to three floors, and the hotel with bungalows sprawled through an open forest with many separate roofs.

The main timbers available for construction were cypress (C. lusitanica, a locally grown exotic conifer) and mangroves (Ceriops tagal and Rhizophera mucronata) and, for large poles, Eucalyptus saligna. Since there were no seasoning kilns, the sawn timber for all purposes was air-seasoned, and much of

---

*Principal lecturer, Department of Civil and Aeronautical Engineering, Royal Melbourne Institute of Technology, Melbourne.

it was not very well seasoned. The problems associated with the emc of 16-18 per cent were not too great, but some troubles were expected in the air-conditioned portions of the hotel, which would have a much lower emc. Facilities for pressure treatment were available for the cypress and saligna, which were treated up-country and shipped 600 km to the coast. This facility was far too expensive, however, to be used for the mangroves. The grading rules were very poor, having been drawn up by the Forest Department without reference to engineering requirements. This was by-passed by writing performance specifications that were included in the contract documents and so over-rode the government-imposed specifications [1]. Strength values were available for cypress and saligna [2]. The saligna values were not the same as those in use in Australia or South Africa, where the same species was grown as an exotic, because growth conditions were different.

Strength values for the mangroves were not available in the year or so between the initial design brief and the start of construction, so a number of poles were collected from along the coast by the Forest Department and tested at the University of Nairobi by the writer [3]. This effort yielded the necessary strength data.

B. Roof coverings

As noted above, the roofs were mangrove pole framing under palm thatch made locally. These roofs had a life of about ten years, after which a maintenance gang was to be sent through to tie up the poles and re-thatch. Traditionally, such poles were tied together with miaa, a string made from a local dwarf palm. Sisal string was substituted to make rather stronger joints, and the writer spent time teaching the roof-makers how to tie better knots. Mangrove poles, though classified as "perishable" with respect to durability, had been reputed over many generations to have long life in roof construction. The only factor that had changed was the introduction in about 1940 of Cryptotermes, which 30 years later had become widespread along the coast. All enquiries indicated that these mangroves were resistant to Cryptotermes. They were known also to be resistant to subterranean termites when used above ground.

The poles of course contained sapwood, but the traditional post-felling treatment included soaking in sea water for some weeks, and there was no evidence of the sapwood being attacked by anything. One minor innovation was the introduction of pre-cast concrete shoes, which were set in concrete members for attaching the mangrove pole structures.

C. Major roof structures

Several areas were much too large to be covered with mangrove poles, and some of these were given primary support with treated saligna poles up to 400 mm in diameter. The poles were cut to length before treatment at the plant, some 800 km away. They were erected by a steel erector using gin poles. Cranes were not available, and even had they been, the contractors' organization was not geared to the rapid erection that would have been concomitant. The ends of many of the poles were cut to receive steel fixings and these cuts, of course, went through the protective coating. There was some end splitting, although not as much as there would have been in a dry climate, which was reduced to some extent by slotting and ring-grooving the ends of the poles. The ends were treated with protective chemicals, which procedure at the time appeared to be valid but in retrospect was probably a waste of time.

D. Wooden dowels

Since one of the major cost components of trusses in East Africa had been the cost of bolts, dowels were considered as an alternative. On this project, the steelwork would inevitably rust unless it was very heavily galvanized and well maintained. In early discussions with the architects, wooden dowels were suggested as likely to be much cheaper and more durable. This was accepted and incorporated into the idiom of the architecture, especially in handrails. Some 10,000 dowels, mostly handmade from mangrove off-cuts, were used. In one structure that was about 13 m in diameter with a centre pole, the rafters were attached to the centre pole with wooden dowels only; and these were proper dowels made from iroko.

E. Seasoning

Poor seasoning was one of the main reasons why architects in Kenya disliked timber. The seasoning defects were irritating and led to high replacement costs. Since the timber industry had had no building experience, it had no understanding of the architects' problems. Carpenters and joiners and technicians were not taught seasoning because the syllabuses did not include this. The response to this was to get builders to sticker-stack timber on site early if theft was not a problem. By this means, 25 mm thick structural timbers would partially season sufficiently so that careful detailing could avert warping problems.

Structural members were made up from 25 mm boards by vertical laminations with nails. This not only solved virtually all the seasoning warp that had previously been such an annoyance but also led to greater structural stability as continuous beams became possible. With joinery timbers, the problem was more difficult. An attempt was made to get joiners to use dowelled joints in place of mortice and tenon joints, which are very sensitive to movement. Timbers with low shrinkage - less than 1 per cent tangential - were used where possible. Perhaps the main innovation was the requirement that the contractors should have on site a moisture meter, and a requirement to this effect was written into the contract documents. This concentrated attention on the need for proper seasoning, with contractors relaying this need back to suppliers and gaining some improvement in quality. It was also found necessary to give gentle briefings to furniture designers and architects on how to detail for movement. It was not considered proper for engineers to instruct architects on their detailing, so some tact was required. Ultimately, there were far fewer failures of table tops etc. and more confidence in the use of timber.

F. Mangrove concrete slab supports

Traditionally, upper-storey floors were made of mangrove poles placed close together, packed with coral lumps and then topped with a lime plaster floor finish. Such a ceiling certainly had character, as did the inevitable non-planar floor. After it had been decided to reproduce this effect, a study was made of the various interactions between mangrove poles and reinforced concrete. The final design had mangrove poles placed touching each other across the short span. These were propped during construction to avoid the characteristically large deflections of the traditional floor. Over them was laid polyethylene sheeting, followed by reinforcement and concrete. After casting, the plastic was burnt off and the soffit oiled. The finished floor relied entirely on the steel reinforcement as the poles were much less stiff than the reinforced concrete. The mode of failure of traditional roofs was decay of the pole ends where they were buried in the walls. In this project, the ends of the poles were left exposed on a ledge. The rooms were air-conditioned to control the insects that would be naturally attracted to holes around the exposed ends.

G. Timber joinery

The architectural profession has to deal with a very wide variety of materials and is traditionally weak on basic science, so engineers often find themselves advising architects on materials. In this case, the main joinery timber was expected to be mvule (Chlorophora excelsa, iroko in West Africa), which was resistant to everything and an excellent joinery timber by international standards. All mvule had been coming from Uganda, but at the time some political problems had halted its export. It was realized early that significant delays could be anticipated, so a start was made on looking for an alternative.

Several species that appeared suitable were found by the writer through the literature, and samples were obtained. The Forest Department told the architects that availability was good, so the architects relaxed. The writer checked up and found that there was indeed an abundance of the timber available as trees. It could not, however, be extracted until after the next rainy season; after conversion and air-seasoning it would be at least nine months before the material could be delivered to the joinery shops, and this was far too late. At about that time, the contractor solved the problem by bringing mvule in from Tanzania, which did not have a large supply and had banned its export to soft currency countries such as Kenya. The point of this comment is that architects, engineers, foresters and millers have very little idea of each others' problems, and communication difficulties are to be anticipated.

H. The contractor

In some countries there is an abundance of subcontractors and the skill of the main contractor lies in their management. In Kenya, as in other developing countries, there are very few subcontractors, so the main contractor needs to engage and supervise in detail a very much wider range of trade skills than would his counterpart in, say, Australia. Thus, a main contractor working in a developing country may have to have more technical skills than a main contractor in an industrialized country. Where special care or site craft skills are necessary to cope with variable products, such as timber in Kenya, designers must be prepared to devote thought to this. (Site craft skills cover the kinds of labour and products that cannot be easily described in specifications as no quality assurance specifications exist, so supervision is mainly subjective and not objective.) One approach to this is to make the specifications more explicit, but this may be more satisfying to the specification writer than to the contractor if the latter does not read English too well. What may happen in practice is that designers and quantity surveyors give much more assistance to the contractor, even advising him when he tenders unrealistically low costs. In return, the contractor may respond to comments on quality that are not explicitly covered in the specifications because there are no relevant standards. Where there is some innovation, this is carefully explained in detail to the builder during tendering and again before construction.

In this project and a number of others where there was a much higher timber content than had normally been the case in East Africa, much time was spent with contractors teaching them about timber, e.g. how to sticker-stack, and an innovative designer in a developing country should expect to have to do this.

I. Conclusion

There was no traditional building culture that related to the functions or scale of modern buildings in Kenya. Such is not the case in South-East Asia, where very rich and ancient cultures are often expressed through buildings. Today many of the materials originally used to construct these buildings are becoming difficult to obtain or very expensive and for this reason there is sometimes a shift away from traditional building idioms. One of the challenges for designers today is to find ways of using more economical materials, such as new species of timber, to maintain and improve traditional cultures as expressed through buildings. Anyone can join the concrete, corrugated iron and coke movement. It takes more skill and dedication to also be able to design in timber, and it is also more satisfying.

References

1. P. A. Campbell, "Performance specifications for the quality control of timber for use in housing in developing countries", World Consultation on the Use of Wood in Housing (Vancouver, 1971).

2. P. A. Campbell and K. Malde, Timber for Building in Tanzania (Tanzania Forest Department, 1971).

3. P. A. Campbell, "Mangrove poles for construction", Occasional Paper No. 7 (University of Nairobi, Department of Civil Engineering, 1973).

VIII. CASE STUDY OF TIMBER CONSTRUCTION: NEW ZEALAND

G. B. Walford*

Introduction

This study describes three examples of timber construction and shows that it is possible to build timber structures economically and achieve a result that is both functional and aesthetically pleasing. It should be emphasized that a structure is considered economical only in relation to the availability and cost of materials and skills at a certain place and time. Another factor that makes comparison difficult is the social or prestige value of a building. For instance, in Auckland, the old Customhouse building of brick and timber construction was strengthened and refurbished in 1982 at a cost of $NZ 3 million, about the same amount as it would have cost to replace the building with a building having six to eight times the earthquake resistance, i.e. built to current structural standards.

The examples presented are as follows:

(a) A farm building incorporating timber portal frames;

(b) A single-storey, 4,526 m^2 warehouse of nailed plywood and sawn timber construction;

(c) A four-storey composite timber and reinforced concrete office building of 3,900 m^2, together with a single-storey trading building of 4,200 m^2.

A. Farm building

1. Structural system

The HB system of timber construction, a proprietary product of A. S. Nicholson and Son, Ltd., of Ottawa, is described briefly in [1]. It consists of structural beams and frames of I-shaped cross-section built up by nailing and/or gluing timber flanges onto a web made of two layers of boards placed at right angles to each other and at 45 degrees to the axis of the members. Figure 50 shows details of a frame and some of the many shapes that have been built using this system. Examples are also given in [2] and in reports originating from the Forest Research Institute at Dehra Dun, India.

The system is by no means new, but few examples are to be seen nowadays. This is probably because plywood provides a better web material, the system is labour-intensive and if the flange-to-web connection is nailed, then creep deformations can be large. Nevertheless, the system has application where sawn timber, nails and labour are the available resources.

---

*Scientist, Forest Research Institute, Rotorua, New Zealand.

- 72 -

Figure 50. HB system of timber construction

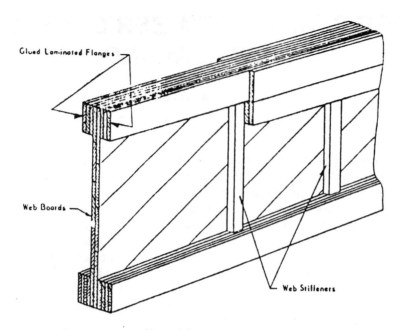

Typical Section of an HB Member

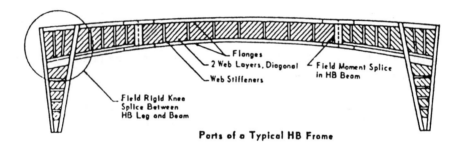

Parts of a Typical HB Frame

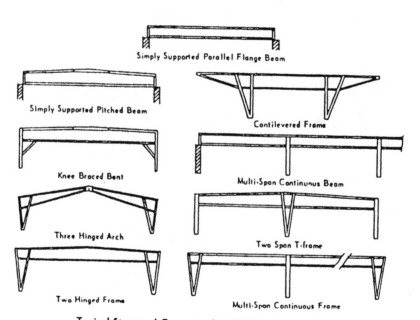

Typical Structural Forms in which HB Members may be Arranged

2. Wool-shed design

The farm building shown in figure 51 is a two-storey wool-shed. This design allows for holding pens beneath and a loading stage at a height convenient for loading bales of wool onto a truck. The frames were built entirely of 25 mm thick timber and were nailed. Although the design specified 100 mm nails at 100 mm centres along the flanges and twice this density in the knee region, far fewer nails were actually driven. The construction procedure for the frames required a flat working surface. In this case, the framing for the wool-shed floor was first erected and then used as a working surface.

Figure 51. Wool-shed with timber portal frames

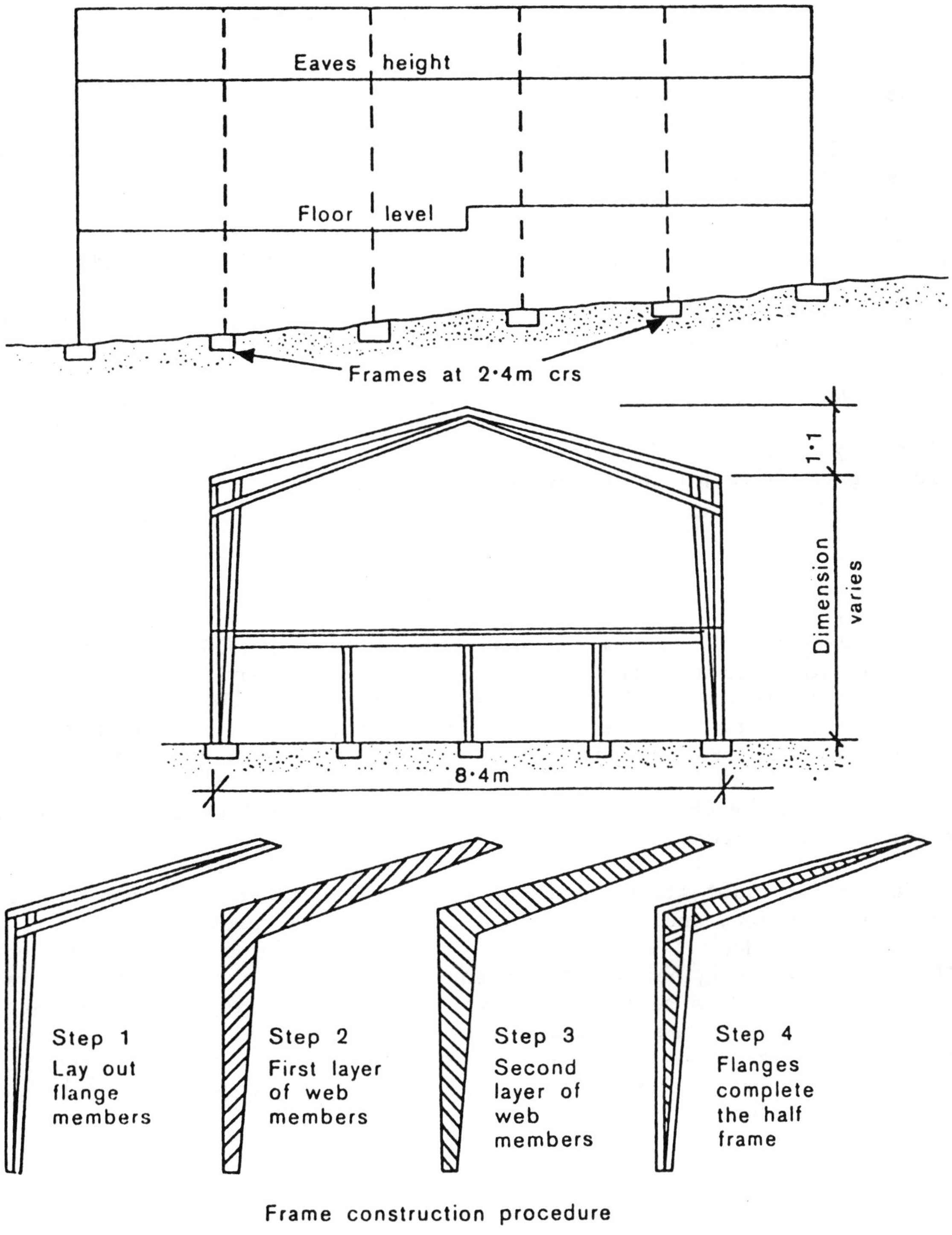
Eaves height
Floor level
Frames at 2·4m crs
1·1
Dimension varies
8·4m
Step 1
Lay out flange members
Step 2
First layer of web members
Step 3
Second layer of web members
Step 4
Flanges complete the half frame

Frame construction procedure

It was found much easier to pour the concrete footings at their correct positions but at whatever height the ground level dictated than to level the site first. The length and taper of the portal legs were varied to allow for the differing levels. The resulting differences in taper were not noticeable.

An alternative design in this case would have used trusses spanning 8.4 m from wall to wall and would have used less timber, but it would have required more attention to bracing against wind loads. The particular advantage of the portal was that roosting spaces for birds could be eliminated and 3 m headroom was available for operating the wool-press.

The analysis and design of these frames is simple:

(a) Assume a span to depth ratio of about 10:1. This determines the depth at mid-span of a beam or at the knee of a portal;

(b) Calculate flange sizes from the direct compression and tension stresses induced by bending moments;

(c) Resolve the shear forces at 45° C to obtain forces in the web members. Usually these will be very lightly stressed;

(d) Resolve the forces in the web members parallel to the flanges and calculate the number of nails required from the allowable nail loads;

(e) Design the knee joint so that both flange members are not discontinuous at the same point. Note the details in steps 1 and 4 in figure 51.

The wool-shed described is an extremely modest example of this system. Larger structures will require splices in the flange members. These can be achieved by making the flange members out of several thicknesses of timber and staggering the butt joints in the individual layers.

B. Warehouse building

1. Description

The warehouse structure consists of nailed plywood box beams, nailed laminated timber columns and nailed plywood roof diaphragms and sheer walls. Figures 52 and 53 show a plan and cross-section of a building that is used for a paper warehousing and distribution operation. Paper is received in bulk form, guillotined into standard sizes, placed on pallets and stored in a rack system for retrieval and dispatch. The incorporated office block has two floors of 600 m^2 each with a timber frame and plywood shear wall system for resisting lateral loads.

The design brief stated that the building should be an economical form of timber construction, and the functions of the various areas dictated the basic layout and roof shape. Walls divided the bulk storage area into two sections with a clear stacking height of 6 m and separated this area from the racking area with storage to a height of 8.3 m; a further wall separated the cart dock and loading area. These internal walls, along with the exterior walls, when lined on both sides made an ideal layout for a shear wall system. The roof-line, although broken into several large panels, provided a reasonable roof diaphragm system.

Figure 52. Plan of a warehouse structural frame

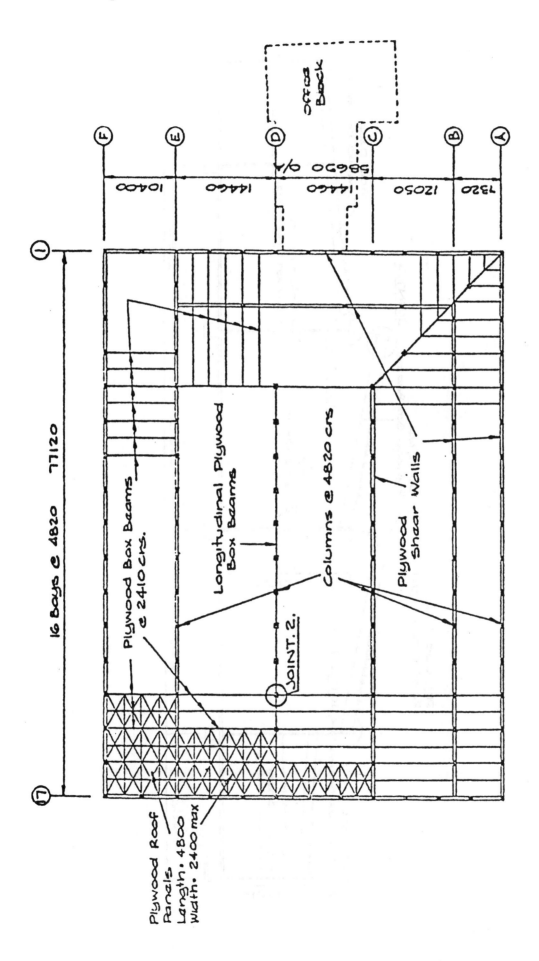

Figure 53. Cross-section of warehouse structural frame

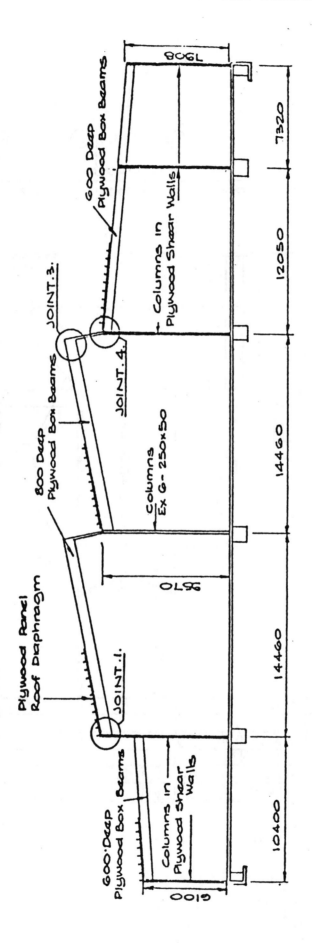

2. Alternatives

Various components were considered:

(a) Trusses were about 10 per cent cheaper than equivalent nailed plywood box beams but were considered undesirable for this application because the accumulation of fine wood fibre would present a fire hazard;

(b) Glulam beams were about 50 per cent more expensive than the plywood box beams;

(c) Steel beams were about 35 per cent more expensive than the plywood box beams and almost 50 per cent more expensive when the cost of fixings to the roof and columns was included.

3. Design philosophy

Wall and ceiling linings that can also act as shear diaphragms are an ideal application for plywood. The additional nailings cost little and allow the use of a pin-jointed beam and column system to support gravity loads.

The selection of building modules had to cater for the following:

(a) The use of whole sheets for linings;

(b) Adequate tolerances in fitting together of components;

(c) Proportioning the various units for economy and ease of handling.

The first two criteria are easy to satisfy, but the selection of spacings to give the best proportions requires considerable care. For example, doubling the box beam spacing to 4,820 mm would use the same amount of material in the beams but increase the purlin size from 125 x 50 mm to 200 or 250 x 50 mm; increasing the depth of the box beams would make them less stable.

Readily available materials were specified throughout. This is important as it is of no use to call for materials that are scarce or of unreasonably high quality. Timber lengths were limited to 4,800 mm and timber thicknesses, to 50 mm. The plywood was 7.5 and 12.5 mm DD grade internally and 12.5 mm C-plugged D grade externally. The columns, beams and roof panels were all prefabricated.

4. Components and joints

The prefabricated components were all fully detailed in order to allow fabrication in a pre-cut factory directly from the drawings. Figures 54 and 55 show typical details.

The columns are assumed to be pin-jointed top and bottom and consist of up to six green-gauged (measured in the unseasoned state) 250 x 50 mm pieces. Three rows of nails fix the laminations tightly together and allow the transfer of gravity and wind uplift loads to the outer pieces for transfer to the baseplates, which are shown in figure 56. The longer columns on the exterior walls were strengthened with steel flitch plates nailed to their sides to resist bending loads due to wind. The horizontal girts are also 250 x 50 mm members, and the plywood lining is nailed directly to these on both sides to form a shear-resisting diaphragm.

- 78 -

Figure 54.   Typical beam and column construction

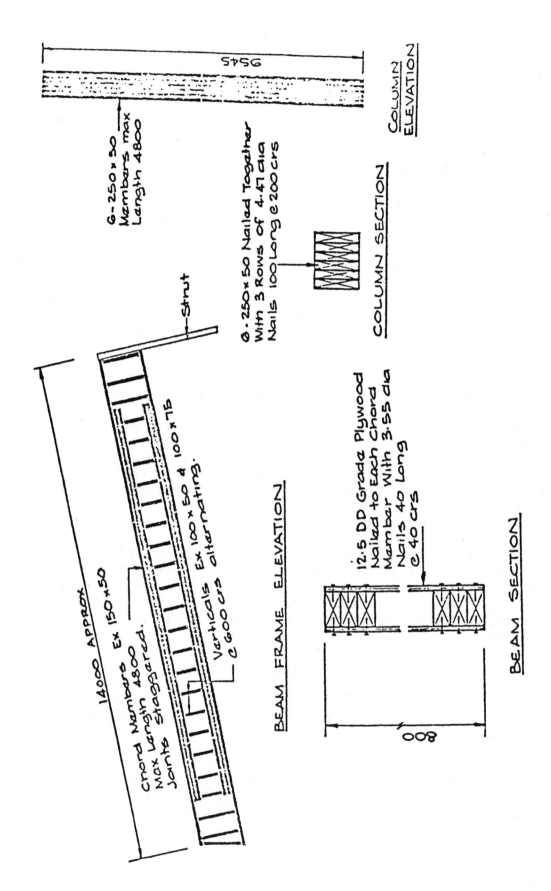

Figure 55. Typical roof panel details

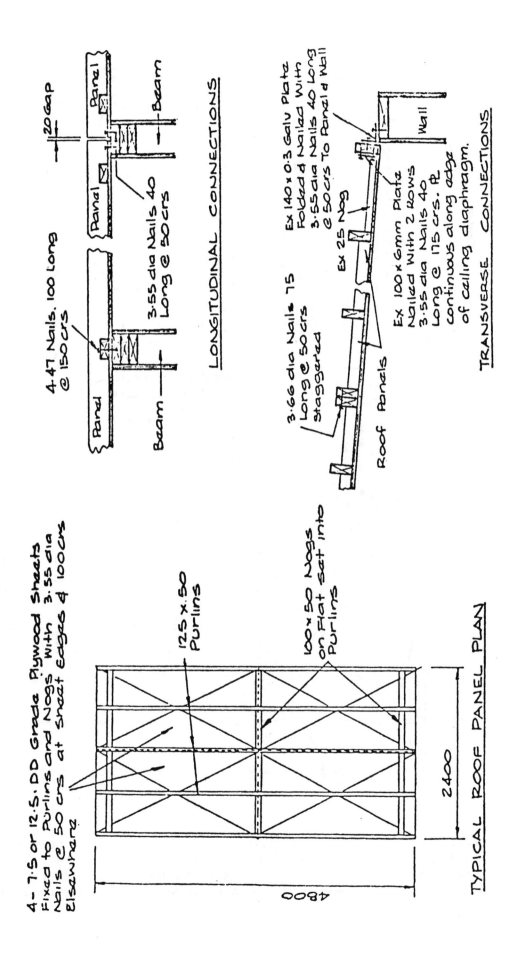

- 80 -

Figure 56.   Typical joint details

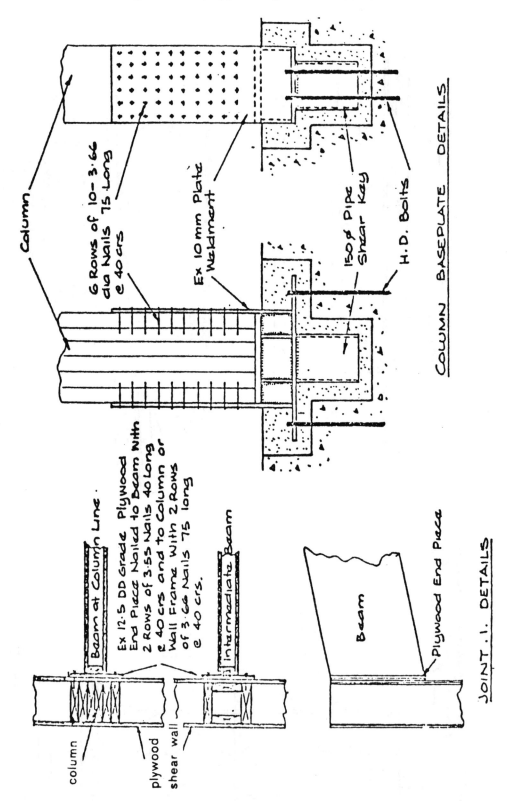

The beams were of conventional plywood box beam construction with details as shown in figure 54. A problem arose with splitting in the 35 mm thick chord members as the design required 3.55 x 40 mm nails at 35 mm centres along both edges of each chord member. This was caused by the use of denser than normal radiata pine and was solved by using radiata from a different forest, increasing the chord thickness to 50 mm and spacing the nails at 40 mm.

The roof panels take advantage of the stressed skin principle, allowing 125 mm deep purlins to span 4.8 m where normally 200 mm deep members would be required.

Joints were designed to be very simple and use nails wherever possible. Figure 56 shows joint 1 details where a plywood end plate is nailed to the end of a beam and to the wall frame or longitudinal beam. The ceiling diaphragm connects the top of the beam to the top of the wall to avoid stressing the nails in withdrawal and pulling the joint apart.

Further joint details are shown in figure 57, where the struts between the rooflights connect to the top of a beam or wall. Again, nails in shear provide the fixing.

5. Problems

The problem of splitting with nails at 10D (ten times diameter) spacing has already been mentioned. This was unusual because radiata pine can usually take nails down to 5D spacings without problems.

The joint 2 detail shows a typical connection in a row of beam-column joints. The beam end fitted tightly against the column, whereas it would have been better to leave a tolerance of 10 mm and provide a ledge to rest the end of the beam on.

Green-gauged timber was specified for the columns and wall girts. It would have been easier to use dry timber: because the timber was partly dry, there were variations in thickness and straightness.

C. Multistorey building

1. Introduction

A new office building has been constructed for the Odlins Group in Petone, New Zealand. Because this firm deals in timber, it wanted the building to be a suitable advertisement for timber. The result was a design that capitalizes on the advantages of timber, avoids its disadvantages and is 10 per cent cheaper than the next most competitive alternative in reinforced con- crete. This economy was achieved by a saving in the cost of making the struc- ture earthquake-resistant owing to the lower dead load of timber construction; by the minimal specification of the timber components, avoiding unnecessary treatment, unnecessarily high grades etc.; and by providing for complete sprinkler protection from fire in the timber design. A further benefit to the client was a saving of 8 months in construction time (12 months compared to 20 for concrete construction).

2. Description

Figure 58 shows an artist's sketch of the office building and trading complex. The octagonal office block has reinforced concrete piles, foundations, floor and lift shafts with a timber gravity-load-resisting system of floors, beams, columns, roof trusses and exterior walls. The trade block has a concrete floor with timber columns supporting timber trusses and is braced by plywood shear walls. Only in 1978 did such construction become permissible. In

Figure 57.   Typical joint details

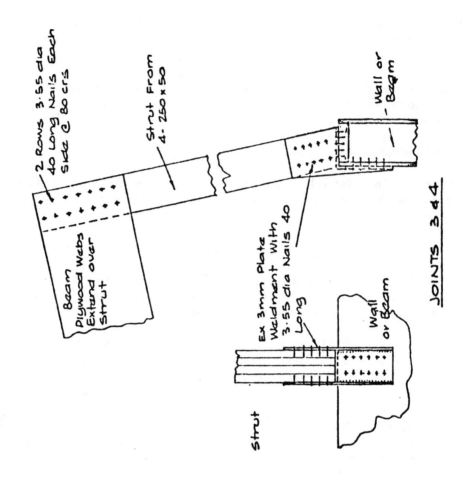

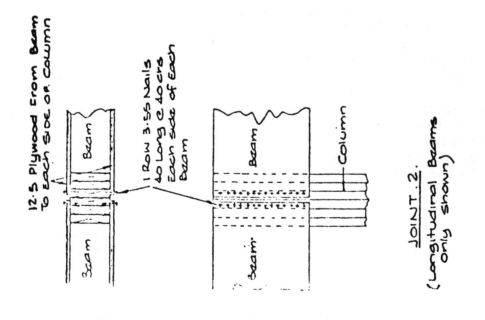

Figure 58. Odlins new complex at Petone

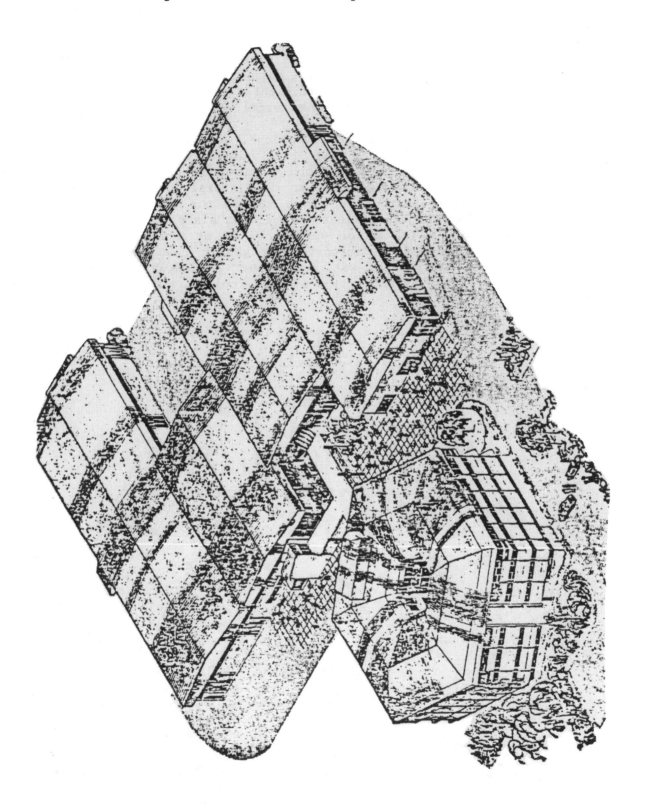

that year, the New Zealand standards on fire-resistant construction were
amended to allow the use of timber construction for buildings up to four
storeys high provided a sprinkler system is installed. This amendment has
allowed a significant increase in heavy timber construction, which had previously been restricted to small buildings with a maximum of two storeys, and
it brings the New Zealand code into line with the Canadian and United States
codes. The building is also sited sufficiently clear of the site boundaries
that no fire rating is required for the external walls.

Because the trade block is of conventional construction, only the office
building will be described. This has three suspended floors of 970 m^2 each
and a plywood-sheathed, prefabricated trussed roof of timber principally supported on heavy timber beams and columns, with lateral loads being resisted by
two reinforced-concrete shear cores, which enclose the stairwell and liftwells
of the building. The suspended floors are glulam slabs 65 mm thick supported
on glulam joists 405 x 144 mm or 405 x 219 mm at 2.5 m centres spanning
6.5 m. The floor joists are supported on glulam beam and column frames
located at the outer perimeter wall, the inner perimeter wall and half-way
between the two. Figure 59 shows typical beam, column, joist and floor dimensions.

Figure 59. First and second floor framing plan

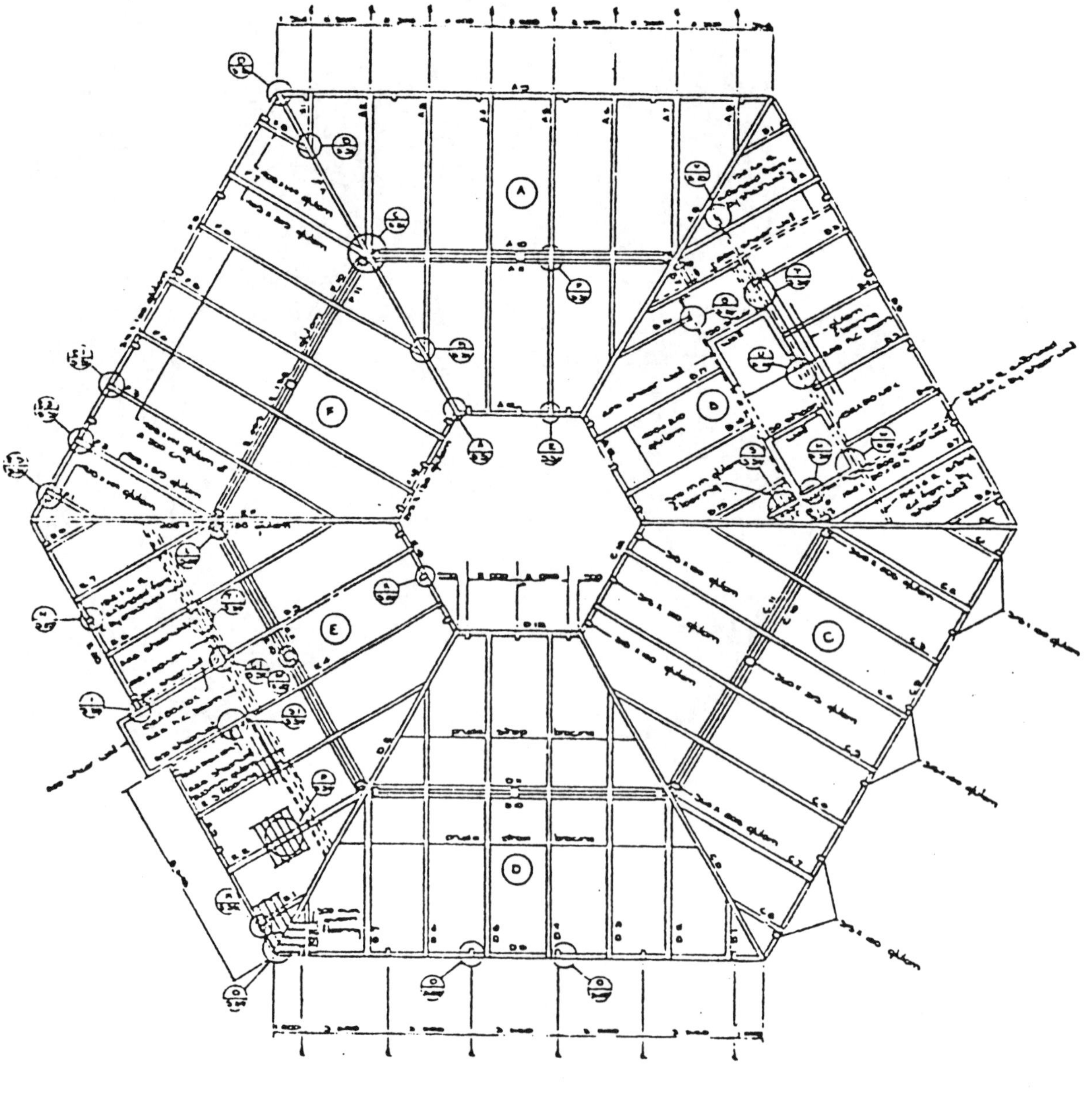

This particular system was adopted for the following reasons:

(a)   Rigid support was preferred to plywood shear walls or a steel frame for the liftwell and the lifting machinery;

(b)   The shear cores localized the lateral elements that resist loading, requiring the floors to act as diaphragms and enabling the timber construction to be of simple post and beam design with simple connections;

(c)   The shear cores could be constructed in advance and would provide support for the timber frame during erection;

(d)   Construction of the shear cores would provide continuity of work on site while the glulam members were being prepared;

(e)   The roof could be completed before the floors were laid, allowing them to be kept dry, which was essential.

3. Joint details

Figure 60 shows that the beam-column joints are simple, giving easy construction and good fire resistance, with gravity loads being taken in direct bearing. Where timber to timber bearing connections were not possible, heavy (10 mm thick) steel brackets were provided in accordance with American Institute of Timber Construction recommendations whereby the joint should not collapse if the steel yields at elevated temperatures in a fire (figures 61 and 62).

All bolt heads were recessed and concealed by timber plugs to give them a fire resistance rating.

The column base fixing was achieved with steel dowels screwed into the end grain of the columns and grouted into ducts in the concrete after the frames had been erected and aligned.

4. Specifications

All glulam members were made from untreated radiata pine of the following grades: Engineering, No. 1 Framing and No. 2 Framing. These correspond approximately to F8, F5 and F4 grades, respectively, in the Australian system. The members were made predominantly of No. 2 Framing grade with a little No. 1 Framing and Engineering grade being used where design stresses dictated. The use of large quantities of low-grade timber was possible because stiffness, not strength, was usually the governing criterion.

Figure 60.   Typical external and internal columns

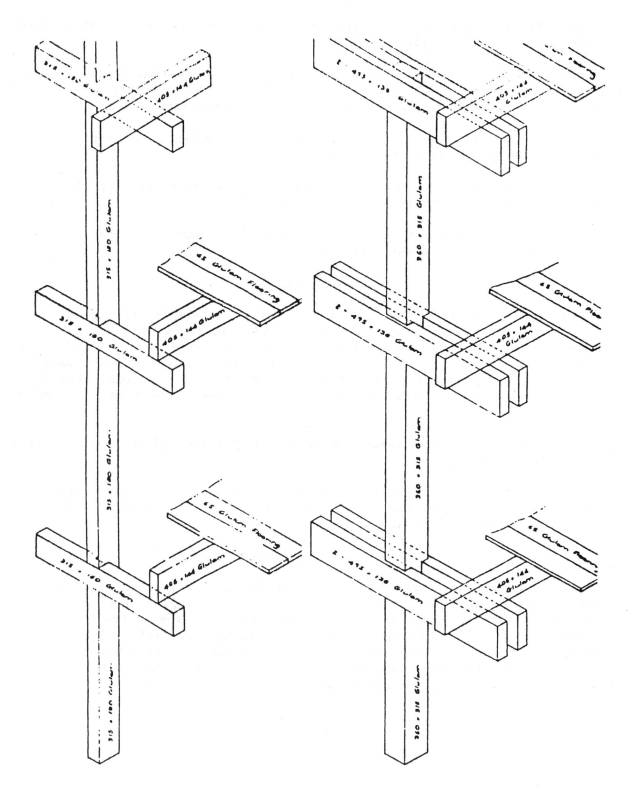

Figure 61. Isometric of exposed bracket, 1:10

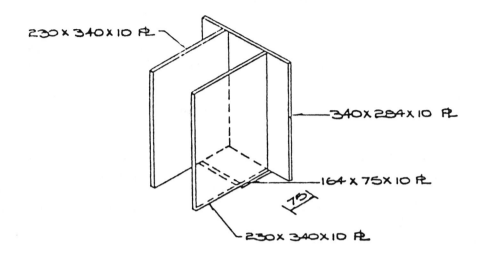

Figure 62. Isometric of concealed bracket, 1:10

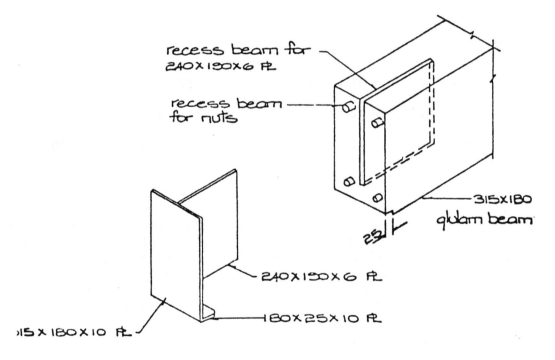

Laminations 45 mm thick were used in all internal members, while 19 mm thick laminations were used for external members in an attempt to reduce splitting owing to changes in the surface moisture content.

Melamine-urea adhesive was specified for internal members, while resorcinol was used in exterior members.

The only preservative treatment given to internal members was to incorporate 0.5 per cent of the insecticide dieldrin in the water-repellent sealer that was applied by brush before the members were erected. This was considered sufficient protection against borer attack; termites are not a problem in New Zealand. For exterior members, a retention of copper-chrome-arsenic preservative salts of 10 kg/m^3 was required. This provides resistance to decay even in ground contact. This was probably an excessively stringent specification as half this retention is sufficient to protect pine timber against decay if it is exposed to the weather and out of contact with the ground.

The surface finish to all internal members was a further coat of water-repellent sealer, then two coats of gloss varnish. External members were finished with primer, undercoat and finishing coats of paint. Particular attention was paid to the abutting surfaces of the main frame members, where an intumescent paint was applied before assembly. This was a precaution against flaming in the event of fire.

5. Glulam costs

On this job, the quotations received revealed that the following savings, expressed as a percentage of the cost, could be made:

Use of untreated in lieu of boron-treated timber	6
Use of melamine-urea instead of resorcinol adhesive	8
Use of No. 2 Framing grade in lieu of No. 1 Framing grade	25
Use of No. 1 Framing grade in lieu of Engineering grade	20
Manufacture of larger volumes of glulam than for one-off jobs	50

D. Conclusion

In New Zealand, both the design of timber structures and expertise in their construction are growing to the point where economically competitive buildings can be built. The vast majority of these are single-storey buildings for agricultural or horticultural enterprises, but multi-storey buildings are also being built. To achieve economical construction and satisfactory performance, it is important that the designer should be aware of both the advantages and disadvantages of timber as a structural material.

References

1. Canadian Institute of Timber Construction, Timber Construction Manual (Ottawa, 1959).

2. R. E. Pearson, N. H. Kloot and J. D. Boyd, Timber Engineering Design Handbook (Carlton, Victoria, Melbourne University Press, 1958).

IX. CASE STUDY OF TIMBER CONSTRUCTION: SOUTH-EAST ASIA

John R. Tadich*

A. Timber, the material

The use of timber as a structural material in larger buildings requires a greater effort on the part of the responsible engineers than the use of materials such as steel and reinforced concrete, which, unlike timber, have infrastructures capable of supplying materials to an engineer's specification. Even Australia, which has a timber industry that can be considered to be cohesive by world standards, could not until recent years supply timber in engineering grades.

In some developing countries, the lack of material standards for timber extends beyond those for durability and strength, to those for the very basic property of sizes. Thus, before starting to design timber structures, it is important to determine the possible sources of the material and ascertain the following details:

(a) Finished timber sizes and corresponding lengths;

(b) Quantities of relevant sizes;

(c) Species;

(d) Availability of quality control and grading standards and ability of suppliers to conform to them.

On many occasions engineers have had to redesign timber structures because the local timber industry could not supply to specification. Wherever possible, the use of large sections of high-grade materials should be avoided, because the larger the section the more difficult it is to achieve the higher grades. Structures should be designed to utilize common sizes and grades.

B. Design concept

Before attempting to conceive the structure of a building, an engineer should determine the skills and infrastructure available to fabricate the components and then erect them. Fundamental considerations such as the type of connectors available influence the conceptual design of timber buildings. When choosing connector types, a number of factors must be taken into account.

1. Possibility of prefabricating components

If there is a timber prefabrication plant within economical transportation distance, many design and fabrication problems can be easily resolved. There are many companies now being established in developing nations to manufacture prefabricated structural components for buildings.

---

*Technical Director, Gang-Nail Australia Ltd., Mulgrave, Victoria.

These plants invariably use multi-tooth connector systems that are backed by the specialist timber engineering services of their manufacturers. Before getting involved in detailed design, contact with one or two of these companies would be invaluable. Most would be able to prepare a feasibility design and a costing for the project. Even though there may not be a prefabrication plant in the immediate area, prefabrication should not be discounted, because on many projects it has been proven economical to transport components hundreds of kilometres. On larger scale projects, prefabricators have equipment that is transportable and can be set up at the job site.

2. Architectural design

Architectural design sometimes dictates the type of connector to be used. For example, in some public buildings where the structure is to be an architectural feature of the building, a large timber section may need to be used, together with connectors such as split rings or shear plates.

3. Cost of connectors

The cost of connectors and the installation of connectors is a very significant cost in timber structures. Since the in-place cost of connectors can vary from 10 to 30 per cent of the cost of the building element, careful analysis of the cost of the various connector types is essential before detailed design. The choice of connector can also influence the volume of timber used in a structure. For example, the use of double top or bottom chords in a truss may be necessary to avoid large, eccentrically loaded joints, whereas a single member may have been adequate.

4. Environment

A corrosive service environment may preclude the use of some types of connectors, e.g. common steel nails, which will quickly corrode and fail. Two types of connectors offer very good corrosion protection:

(a) Ceramic connectors, which are shear connectors made from steatite. If used with brass or stainless steel bolts, they provide good protection. These connectors have been used extensively for cooling towers in large air-conditioning plants;

(b) Stainless steel multi-tooth connectors are available on special request from some manufacturers. These connectors are obviously much more expensive than standard galvanized connectors and should only be used in extreme circumstances. Galvanized connectors provide satisfactory service in most conditions.

5. Connector installation costs

As the cost of connector installation forms a significant portion of the cost of fabricating building components, it greatly influences the layout of the building and, hence, its overall economics.

If the installation cost is small and it is possible to design lightweight elements, these elements can be placed at very close centres, dramatically reducing the cost of secondary structural members.

For example, multi-tooth trusses supporting large-span, heavyweight tiled roofing with a ceiling at bottom chord level, would be placed at 600 or 900 mm centres using standard battens fixed directly to the chords. The alternative would be to use bolted or split-ring trusses at 1,800 or 2,000 mm centres with underpurlins and intermediate rafters and ceiling joists, which would add considerably to the costs of material and on-site labour.

C. Important features of connectors

Connector performance is covered in the chapter "Timber connectors" of Strength Characteristics and Design, the fourth volume in this collection, and will not be repeated here. However, it may be useful to point out pitfalls in the use of some connectors.

1. Split rings

Split rings are so named because they are in fact rings that have a split (figure 63). The function of the split is to accommodate timber shrinkage. During installation, the grooves should be formed so that the connector is sufficiently expanded when placed into the groove to prevent the ring from completely closing when the timber has shrunk.

Figure 63.   Split ring

Some contractors use sections of pipe in lieu of split rings. This practice of course restrains timber shrinkage and induces splitting, which could cause major problems. It also increases joint slippage as the parallel sides of pipe do not take up the groove tolerance as does the tapered section of the split ring.

2. Multi-connector joints

Extreme care should be taken to avoid joint details that restrain timber shrinkage. For example, the use of bolts spaced across the grain invites disaster (figure 64).

- 92 -

Figure 64. Because timber shrinks in size across the grain and
not longitudinally when it dries, internal stresses are
induced that can cause severe splitting

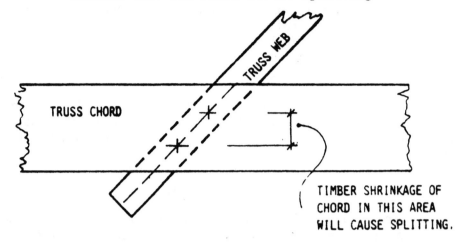

TIMBER SHRINKAGE OF
CHORD IN THIS AREA
WILL CAUSE SPLITTING.

3. Load perpendicular to the grain

Connections should never be designed so as to develop tension perpendicular to the grain without taking some precaution against splitting. A common
case is the support of standard trusses by girder trusses in complex roof
designs.

The girder bracket connection here is always reinforced by a multi-tooth
connector placed either side of the bracket to distribute tension perpendicular forces across the face of the girder bottom chord (figure 65).

Figure 65. Multi-tooth connector prevents splitting due to tension
perpendicular to the grain

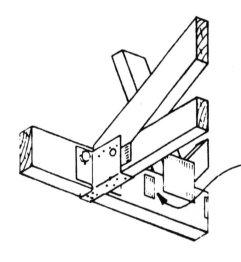

MULTI-TOOTH CONNECTOR TO PREVENT
SPLITTING DUE TO PRESENCE OF
TENSION PERPENDICULAR TO GRAIN.

4. Installation of multi-tooth connectors

Most multi-tooth connectors are designed to be pressed into the timber by means of substantial hydraulic or impact presses. Such connectors are readily recognizable as the teeth protrude perpendicularly to the plate (figure 66). It is possible to drive this type of connector into soft timber on site with special hammers. However, the hammers may not be capable of developing the published design loads, so the practice should be avoided.

Figure 66. Factory-fixed multi-tooth connector

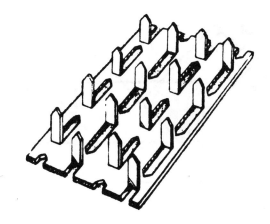

There are multi-tooth connectors that are designed to be installed with a hammer, e.g. Teco nail-on plates and Tylok connectors (figure 67).

Figure 67. Site-fixed multi-tooth connectors

TYLOK PLATE

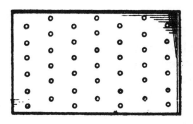

TECO NAIL-ON-PLATE

5. Design of multi-tooth connector joints

Multi-tooth connector joints should be designed so that compression loads are always taken by a timber to timber bearing (figure 68). The joints should always be arranged so that timber shrinkage does not cause compression loads to be shed to connectors (figure 69), which could cause buckling of the plates and significantly reduce strength.

Figure 68. Typical joint arrangement to restrain the compression
load via the end bearing

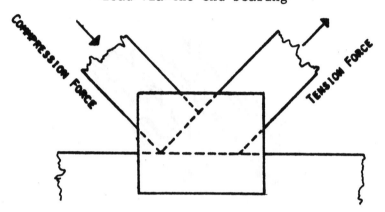

Figure 69. The shrinkage of web 1 will cause the multi-tooth connector
to buckle and will reduce the strength of the joint

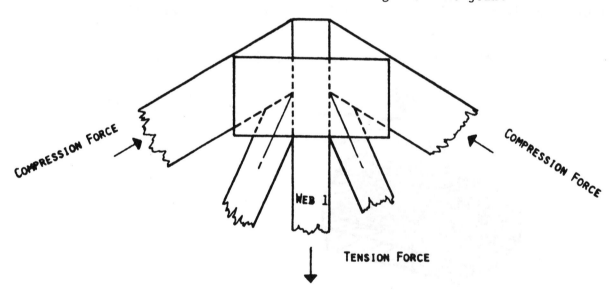

D. Erection and bracing

The author has found that most of the problems in timber structures occur during the erection stage or are due to poorly installed temporary or permanent bracing.

1. Erection

Erection problems on larger structures such as factory buildings seem to revolve around the lack of expertise in the erection of timber structures. Rigging crews have had much experience with steel and tend to handle timber in the same manner. Large-span timber members are much more flexible than similar steel members, however, and they require considerably more care. Gang-Nail Australia Ltd. always spells out erection procedures in the design documents. These instructions include instructions on lifting and on temporary bracing.

The usual technique is to stand groups of trusses on the ground, temporarily brace them together and lift them as a group. Alternate purlins may be fixed, reducing the number of man-hours for fixing ancillaries in the elevated position and also significantly reducing the cost of crane hire.

2. Bracing

A number of different techniques can be used, the choice largely depending on truss spacing:

(a) For small structures, i.e. those less than 13,000 mm, where trusses are placed at relatively close centres, diagonal bracing in the plane of the top chord is generally adopted (figure 70);

(b) For large spans and wider spaced trusses, special prefabricated bracing trusses or on-site bracing bays are used, as was the case for the open shed at Temerloh (see section F.2). On long buildings it is good practice to include intermediate braced panels, even though the panels at each end may carry the required load. As with long buildings, it is possible to have sufficient slip at joints of the members that tie each end together, which would allow large buckles to develop between braced bays.

Figure 70. Typical bracing for closely spaced trusses,
up to 13,000 mm span

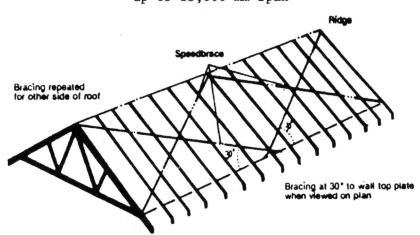

E. Economical building layout

A little time spent during design on determining the most economical layout for a building can lead to a considerable saving in costs. For example,
in an open industrial or agricultural building, the purlins are a major cost
item. Therefore, trusses should be spaced at centres to allow the use of a
common size at its maximum span, preferably allowing the trusses to span continuously over three supports. In turn, the spacing of the purlins themselves
must be examined, because wide spacings increase the top chord size. Consider
varying purlin spacing in critical top chord panels.

Truss spacings for multi-tooth trusses are generally as follows:

Roofing	Ceiling	Spacing (mm)
Steel sheet	No	2,000-4,000
Corrugated asbestos cement sheet	No	2,000-3,600
Steel sheet	Yes	900-1,800
Corrugated asbestos cement sheet	Yes	900-1,800
Concrete tiles	Yes	600-1,200

Since the cost of labour for the manufacture of multi-tooth connector
trusses is minimal compared to that for other types, it is not economical to
use large members and space the trusses at wide centres. It is more economical to use two trusses at closer centres and reduce ancillary member sizes.

Figure 71 gives approximate economical spans for common truss shapes.

F. Examples of timber structures

1. Lee Sang Lon truss plant

The Lee Sang Lon truss plant is an 18,000 mm arch structure utilizing
space columns. It is characterized by the following:

(a) Very small timber sizes, 125 x 50 top and bottom chords;

(b) T-shaped stiffener or bottom chord to give additional lateral stiffness;

(c) Staggered bolts at footing to column connection to reduce the ten-
dency to split. Possibly Gang-Nail connector should have been used here to
prevent splitting;

(d) Pole-type reinforced concrete footing.

2. Open shed at Temerloh, Malaysia

The shed at Temerloh is a 24,000 x 73,000 mm open building. Trusses and
columns have been designed as rigid elements to restrain lateral movement.
Wind trusses were used to restrain the trusses between columns from lateral
movement. The truss was manufactured in two sections and spliced on site
using timber splice plates and bolts. There was minimal use of steel brackets.

Figure 71. Common truss configurations and their approximate span range. In the starred examples, the number of bays can be varied according to truss span

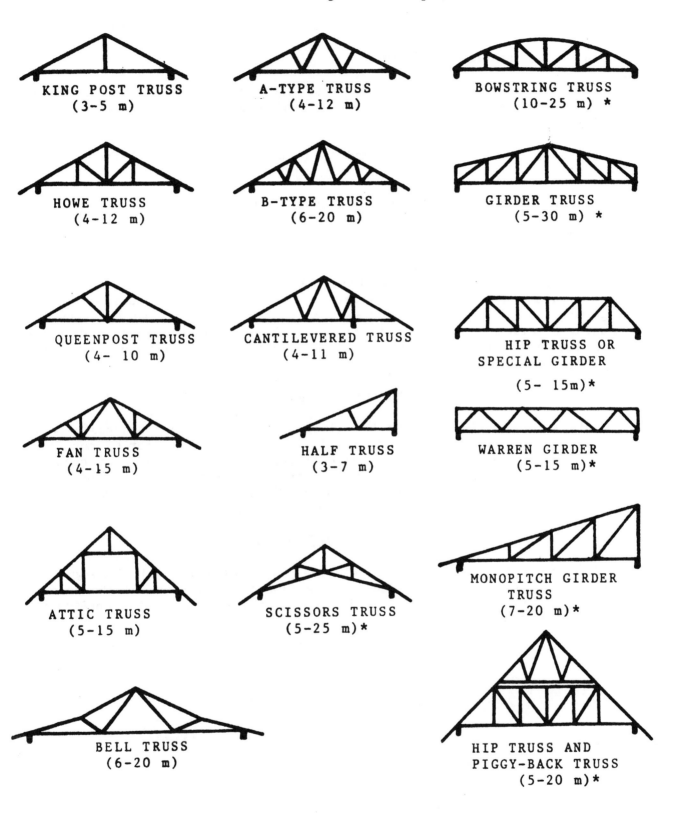

KING POST TRUSS
(3-5 m)

A-TYPE TRUSS
(4-12 m)

BOWSTRING TRUSS
(10-25 m) *

HOWE TRUSS
(4-12 m)

B-TYPE TRUSS
(6-20 m)

GIRDER TRUSS
(5-30 m) *

QUEENPOST TRUSS
(4- 10 m)

CANTILEVERED TRUSS
(4-11 m)

HIP TRUSS OR
SPECIAL GIRDER

(5- 15m)*

FAN TRUSS
(4-15 m)

HALF TRUSS
(3-7 m)

WARREN GIRDER
(5-15 m)*

ATTIC TRUSS
(5-15 m)

SCISSORS TRUSS
(5-25 m)*

MONOPITCH GIRDER
TRUSS
(7-20 m)*

BELL TRUSS
(6-20 m)

HIP TRUSS AND
PIGGY-BACK TRUSS
(5-20 m)*

3. Malaysian community development project at Subang Jaya

Typical low-rise housing project

The low-rise housing at Subang Jaya is characterized by the following:

(a) Close spacing of 600 mm;

(b) The top chords act as rafters, with tile battens fixed directly. The bottom chords act as ceiling joists, with asbestos cement sheet fixed directly;

(c) Top chord bracing is fixed to restrain the top chord from lateral buckling;

(d) Vertical cross-bracing over internal supports.

Typical shop-houses

Small, complex structures such as these shop-houses with bell-shaped roofs can be economical using prefabricated timber trusses. Efficient production techniques using computer systems can be employed to produce structural design and fabrication details automatically. Projects such as this one for community development can be assisted by local fabrication plants or directly by manufacturers of multi-tooth connectors, using their computer system for structural designs.

4. Straits Timber Products factory

This structure demonstrates how timber can be used very successfully in conjunction with other building materials, in this case reinforced concrete, to achieve maximum economy and serviceability. It used reinforced concrete columns and perimeter beams, with 18,000 mm clear span timber trusses. The large span trusses were closely spaced at 1,800 mm. This building was so successful that this first stage was repeated three times.

5. French trade building at Kuala Lumpur

The French trade building is relatively complex and required large open areas. It was originally intended to be a temporary building, so the cost of construction was very critical. It is also a good example of the application of a parallel chord truss.

X.   STRESS GRADES AND TIMBER CONSTRUCTION ECONOMIES, EXEMPLIFIED BY THE UNIDO PREFABRICATED TIMBER BRIDGE

C. R. Francis*

Introduction

The UNIDO modular prefabricated bridge was designed in Kenya in 1973 by James E. Collins as a forest access bridge. From 1975 to 1977 a UNIDO project allowed Mr. Collins to develop the design. The system now covers stress grades from F4 to F34 and 12 different design loadings. The design was done in accordance with AS 1720, Timber Engineering Code. UNIDO has published a comprehensive manual (UNIDO/IO/159-163) in English; distribution is limited.

The bridge consists of a nail-laminated deck platform supported on 45° Warren girders. The Warren girders may number from two to ten across the bridge, and the span may reach 30 m. The girders are composed of 3 m long truss units joined by steel spigot and socket end pieces and mild-steel-pinned bottom chords.

The bridge is designed for prefabrication in a workshop and site assembly using only hammer and nails for major components. A launching system using two derricks and a cable-way has been devised. No major plant except a mobile welder is required for assembly, but an electric generator and portable power tools speed the work considerably.

The writer inherited the bridge project as part of an expanded project in Kenya in 1979, and in 1981 he made brief visits to Honduras and to Madagascar to advise on the initiation of bridge projects there, using the UNIDO system. Since 1983, he has also been involved in UNIDO bridge projects in Bhutan and Dominica. (Other projects have introduced the system into Bolivia, Chile, Ecuador, El Salvador, Nicaragua, Panama and Peru. The International Labour Organisation (ILO) used the system for a multi-span bridge in Malawi. The Oversees Development Authority (United Kingdom of Great Britain and Northern Ireland) built one in Cameroon and the Government of Austria had one built near Vienna.)

The countries generally receive advice on workshop, manpower and material requirements for the programme. The work is usually carried out in four stages:

(a) Ascertain the required bridging programme and design loadings;

(b) Determine timber characteristics and availability;

(c) Determine the annual requirements for trusses and thus for timber and steel quantities;

---

*Chief Technical Adviser for UNIDO Project DP/SRL/79/053, Research and Development for the Utilization of Rubberwood and Coconut Wood.

(d) Determine the necessary facilities for fabrication and erection.

The key stage in this series is (b). Timber strength and quality largely determine the magnitude of stages (c) and (d) and may also feed back to stage (a). Timber strength, i.e. the F rating, is of great importance, but so also are presentation and availability.

Figure 72 has been prepared from the tables contained in the UNIDO report referred to above, for HS20* vehicle loading. Examination of this figure reveals three interesting facts:

(a) The weakest timbers, say up to F7, have only about half the span capacity of the strongest, with an absolute span limit of 15-18 m;

(b) For a particular span, about twice as many trusses are needed with weak timber than with strong timbers;

(c) No great advantage is gained by using timber stronger than F11.

For economic construction, the stress grading problem simplifies to finding a source of timber of a grade not weaker than F11 or, second best, not weaker than F7. More precise identification is not really required. With this design there is no advantage in insisting on, for example, F17, which could well be the case if some old-fashioned hardwood specifications were to be followed.

A. Presentation

The timber industries of the two countries visited, Honduras and Madagascar, are at opposite ends of the spectrum of sophistication in developing countries. For years Honduras has supplied pitch pine (P. carribea and P. oocarpa) to the market in the southern United States. Export-oriented mills are capable of presenting timber having high standards of dimensional tolerance and grade uniformity to United States commercial standards. In Madagascar, timber is available only in 4 m and 6 m lengths, roughly handhewn and, if hardwood, described simply as bois du forêt, with no species separation or grading.

The writer was very impressed by the Honduran pine. Large, perfectly clear timbers were common. Test results and application of (United States) Southern pine grade stresses indicated at least F14, more probably F17, for structural grades. However the timber was available only in American sizes, where the actual thickness of scantlings is 0.5 in. under nominal size. The designs for the bridge called for 55 mm (2 in.) thick timber. Some brief calculations indicated that F11 stresses both in bending and joint details should not be exceeded with scant timber of F14 and better, provided the "dense" United States qualification is complied with.

The problems in Madagascar were more serious. Most of the available timber was a dense red eucalyptus species; there was also a small quantity of less dense yellowish timber. The eucalyptus was most likely E. robusta;

---

*Like H20, referred to later on, a rating of the American Association of State Highway and Transport Officials (AASHTO).

Figure 72.   Bridge construction, HS20 design load

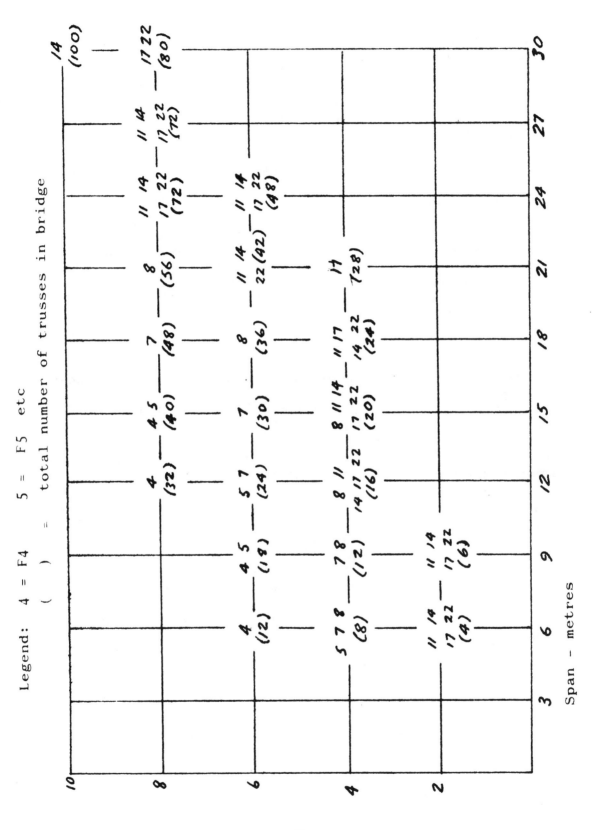

flotation experiments in a tumbler of water showed densities of around 0.9. It was generally clear and straight-grained, so with some on-site selection, it could easily qualify as F17. However, the dimensions available were narrower and thicker than those called for in the design. The only major woodworking machine available was a large overhand planer, and with this it was possible to produce timber 6-7 cm thick and 20-23 cm wide.

The design called for nail-laminated diagonals and king posts, but with only 10 cm nails available it was considered that there would be insufficient point penetration. Also, a major effort would have been needed to reduce the timber to 5 cm thickness.

The trusses were redesigned on the basis of a single 6.5 cm diagonal and king post. With these size and fastening length reductions it was decided that F11 design tables would be adequate for an H20 load.

It is very difficult to compare the costs in different countries. In Kenya, a preliminary estimate would be about 4,400 Kenyan shillings per metre for a four-girder bridge. No cost estimates were prepared by the writer in Honduras or Madagascar. In Madagascar, a peak truss production rate of eight per day was reached with a 10-man gang, but when other work is being done, an average of six would be more reasonable. In Honduras, planning was done on the basis of four trusses per day with six men, but the writer does not know what the subsequent experience was.

Two important lessons can be learned from this bridge experience:

(a) Labour and material quantities can be quite dramatically reduced by relatively small jumps in the F range;

(b) Departures from specified sizes may make it necessary to downgrade the timber to achieve the required structural strength.

B. Relationship between cost and strength

The preceding section was concerned with a predetermined complete design. Given the data contained in figure 72 or similar data for other design loads, a complete estimate can be made for any timber stress grade. This section will explore the more general relationship between strength and cost.

The engineering design process in timber generally takes place in the following sequence:

(a) Specification of architectural requirements: span, spacing, loading;

(b) Selection of structural solutions: beam, truss, arch;

(c) Selection of the material type: scantling, light glulam, heavy glulam;

(d) Calculation of the necessary sections;

(e) Detailing.

At the end of step (d), preliminary estimates may be made and steps (b), (c) and (d) may be repeated in various systems and materials.

In timber design, with its largely rectangular sections, step (c) is the critical one, since the material type largely fixes the breadth of the sections owing to the limited range of commercially available timber sizes.

In the design of a beam, using conventional engineering symbols,

$$f = \frac{M}{Z} = \frac{6M}{bd^2} = \frac{K}{d^2}$$
$$d = \frac{K}{\sqrt{f}}^2 \tag{1}$$

where f is stress, M is bending moment, Z is section modulus, b is breadth and d is depth.

Timber is sold by volume. In two different solutions to the same problem, to have the same cost (PbdL, where P is price per unit and L is length):

$$P_1 bd_1 L = P_2 bd_2 L \tag{2}$$

This is not absolute, since the breadth is only more or less fixed at design step (b), but it is certainly more constant than the depth, which is what we find in design step (d).

Substituting equation (1) in equation (2),

$$P_1 b \frac{K_2 L}{\sqrt{F_1}} = P_2 b \frac{K_2 L}{\sqrt{F_2}}$$

Cancelling and rearranging,

$$P_1/P_2 = (F_1/F_2)^{1/2} \tag{3}$$

A very large number of beam designs are limited by deflection considerations, so that the deflection to span ratio does not exceed a standard value. In this case, identical reasoning using I (moment of inertia) = $bd^3/12$ leads to

$$P_1/P_2 = (E_1/E_2)^{1/3} \tag{4}$$

Equation (4) also covers the case of laterally restrained columns that are designed to an Euler-type formula, such as truss top chords.

Given a price list of timbers of various species and grades and a table of design stresses, a designer can rank various timbers as good or bad structural buys, at least in general terms, by working between the limits set by equations (3) and (4) and bearing in mind the assumptions made in their derivation.

XI. EFFICIENT TIMBER STRUCTURES USING METAL CONNECTORS

E. E. Dagley*

A. Modern timber connectors

Throughout history, before welded and riveted structural steel began to be used, heavy timber was a common construction material. With the advent of steel, timber was replaced for several reasons, not the least of these being that it could no longer compete economically. The problem lay not in the material itself, but in the methods of connecting it. The joints were usually the weakest parts of the structure. To make sufficiently strong joints generally required lapping and overlays of timber, leading to uneconomic use and the understressing of the timber in the balance of the structure.

The solution to these problems is only about 25 years old. It came with the development of gluing techniques and finger jointing and parallel with that, the development of proprietory metal fastenings, in particular toothed metal plate connectors.

B. Structural timber design

Once the rules of structural design are known, the process is straightforward, but the designer's responsibility does not end there. If timber is to be used and its many advantages to be maximized, the following must be planned for at the design stage:

(a) Site fastenings that are cheap and efficient;

(b) Structurally sound but simple bracing systems. Large timber structures are not easy to brace, but simple techniques are now available;

(c) Safe, quick and efficient erection.

C. Modern mechanical fasteners

In times past, timber was generally fastened by means of dowels, bolts, screws, nails etc. or by methods such as dovetailing, mortising etc. The resultant joints were weak compared with the design strength of the timber member; they were also subject to slip and, in some cases, were a slow and expensive exercise.

Modern mechanical fasteners have overcome all of these disadvantages. They are generally highly developed, proprietory items that possess several advantages:

(a) They efficiently use the full timber strength;

---

*Managing Director, Gang-Nail New Zealand Ltd., Auckland.

(b) They do not slip;

(c) They are quick to use;

(d) They are cheap;

(e) In many cases, they virtually weld the timber. Using tooth-plate or nail-on connectors, especially in soft woods, the joint can be made the strongest part of the structure.

D. Building requirements

The designer must ensure that many requirements are satisfied. The most important can be summarized as follows:

(a) The building must have structural integrity. It must be capable of withstanding all possible load combinations;

(b) It should be capable of completion as economically as possible. In a timber-framed building, the designer should ensure that the timber, the fastenings, the labour etc. are being used efficiently;

(c) The building should be as aesthetically pleasing as possible. The principles of architecture should be applied to ensure an attractive result;

(d) It should be durable, in keeping with the life-span planned for it.

Mechanical fastenings have been widely used in New Zealand in the last two decades. Mechanically fastened timber structures have proved to be versatile and attractive as well as economical. They are easy to erect and structurally superior. They exhibit, as well, good fire performance (in contrast to fire resistance) and are both corrosion-resistant and energy-efficient. They can, moreover, be easily interfaced with other materials such as steel and concrete.

E. Site fixings

In New Zealand, heavy structural nail-on techniques have been developed that have allowed Gang-Nail New Zealand Ltd. to supply and erect very large timber structures. Nail-on plate punched in 1.2 mm, 2.0 mm, 3.0 mm and 5.0 mm thicknesses can be cut and fabricated to make a wide variety of brackets and fixings. It is used at the knee and apex of portal frames, for connecting timber to other structural materials such as steel or concrete and for the on-site splicing of large truss components.

F. Bracing

It has been found almost necessary to fully brace the roof components on the ground before erecting them. To do this, Gang-Nail-connected panel or K-braces are used, so that the truss groups are fully assembled and braced before erection.

The roof diaphragm is then often braced using comparatively light metal strap, called "strip brace", tensioned with a convenient high-speed adjustable clip device. Because the strip brace has a capacity loading of only about 8 kN, a number of parallel strips are often used to develop the bracing loads required. This has been found to be the quickest and most economical method.

G. Erection

The trusses are spaced on the ground to their relative final positions. They are then braced in groups of between two and six trusses. While still on the ground, the final bracing is fully installed together with the purlins, the roof services and walkways and often also the roof sheathing.

The nail-on brackets or stirrups at the top of the columns are already in place, and one or more cranes then lift the roof sections. Trusses having free spans of less than 12.0 m do not usually require cranes: provided experienced workmen are on site, they can be lifted into place singly and often by hand. No mechanical lifting is required for small trusses.

Trusses having a free span of over 15.0 m become an engineering exercise, and over 20.0 m free span, the above-described techniques, or equivalent methods, must be used to avoid a collapse during erection.

H. Ganglam

The Ganglam technique entails building up very large timber beams and other components using tooth-plate connectors.

Shorter and smaller members are first laminated end-to-end to obtain the required lengths. The timber used is generally 50 mm thick, and the longer members are then edge-laminated up to any required width, but commonly 600 mm and more.

These 50 mm thick "planks" are then "slabbed" together to produce the required design thickness for the composite beam, usually up to 200 mm or even more. The planks are commonly nailed together where the interface shear requirements are low, such as for a simple beam. However, the interface shear requirements can be higher, as for a column, or can be extremely high, as for a laminated girder.

In these cases, heavy nailing or bolting is required. Where very heavy compression loads are to be carried, special nail-on members are designed or the member is held straight by edge trusses or other means.

I. Curved arches

A special form of Ganglam was introduced in New Zealand in the early 1980s. Thin laminates, usually 50 x 25 mm, are curved to the required shape and the required number are laid up, face to face. Tooth-plate connectors are then driven into the edge faces to carry the interface shear between the laminates. The arch retains its shape when released, and if correctly designed, it is capable of withstanding the necessary design loads.

XII. TIMBER CONSTRUCTION IN DEVELOPING COUNTRIES

C. R. Francis*

The author has had personal experience in five developing countries, which range widely in location, climate and history. However, they all take rather similar approaches to the utilization of timber for structural purposes and have experienced similar problems.

A. Degree of utilization

Aside from its use to build shanties, timber is generally used only for roof framing or, sometimes, for first-floor beams in high-quality housing. Roof framing is heavy and widely spaced; lightweight, trussed rafters are virtually unknown. There may be some use of standard prefabricated buildings or components. There is no use of component systems, e.g. trussed rafters pre-designed and prefabricated to individual architectural requirements, or of standard-spaced, stud-framed wall sections. There are three reasons for this pattern of utilization:

(a) The lack of accurately dimensioned timber;

(b) Ignorance of a particular approach or the inability to adapt it to local circumstances;

(c) The lack of appropriate design codes. Examples of this include insistence on the use of European loadings, which include snow loads, for tropical roof design. In one country, stud-framed walls are apparently not allowed since the load of the studs on the bottom plate would exceed the timber stresses allowed by German standards that were imported in the mid-1920s.

B. Preservation

The lack of preservation severely limits the availability of timber. The general pattern, which also applies to New Zealand and Australia, is that the once-abundant supply of durable species is now exhausted, or rapidly becoming so.

In New Zealand and Australia the shortfall was made good by preserving non-durable timber, notably radiata pine. One project worked on by the author centred on the boron treatment of otherwise useless rubber wood, which is extremely prone to Lyctus attack. Some interesting statistics from a large group of companies involved in the business of preserving wood are shown in table 17.

Some of the data are of doubtful interpretation, but they do show a vast imbalance between developed and developing countries. Also, this is only one group of companies, albeit the major one. The data show clearly the gap

---

*Chief Technical Adviser for UNIDO Project DP/SRL/79/053, Research and Development for the Utilization of Rubberwood and Coconut Wood.

between an intensely preservation-conscious country like New Zealand and third world countries with millions of people per preservation plant.

Table 17. Number of pressure treatment plants in relation to population a/

Country/region	No. of pressure plants	Population (millions)	No. of people per plant (millions)
Great Britain	192	55.9	0.29
New Zealand	124	3.1	0.025
South Pacific	12	0.5	0.041
Singapore, Sri Lanka, Indonesia, Philippines, Taiwan Province and Thailand	54	204.1	3.8
Malaysia	87	12.3	0.1414
India	150	605.8	4
Turkey	3	39.2	13
Scandinavia	46	22.1	0.48
Australia	114	13.5	0.1184
Papua New Guinea	3	2.8	0.933
Canada	20	22.9	1.14

a/ Information available when the workshop was held.

Sound preservation practices are the single most important factor in the establishment and acceptance of timber construction. The main inhibiting factor does not appear to be the direct cost of the plant or chemicals or the lack of skilled personnel to run it. Rather it is the shortage of working capital to cover the cost of drying the wood to ready it for pressure treatment or of storage time for diffusion treatment. The shortage of working capital similarly inhibits drying, not only for structural work but also for furniture and joinery.

C. Skills, training, tools

All the wood-using developing countries appear capable of good standards of craftsmanship in furniture and joinery using hand tools and simple machines. The use of portable power tools and four-sided planers is rare. Timber that is accurately surfaced to standard dimensions is almost totally lacking. Practices with machines are extremely dangerous: saws are used without guards or riving knives, planers and spindle moulders without guards. Moreover, unacceptably dangerous work situations have been observed in countries where health and safety procedures have not been formalized.

A major problem is teaching illiterate workmen to measure. In these circumstances, wide use should be made of gauges and templates.

For construction work, the most useful tools are the radial-arm saw and the portable circular saw. Used intelligently, these can speed up work and also achieve better precision than hand tools. However, instruction in their safe and efficient use is essential.

In order of importance, the four things that need to be done to promote the use of structural timber are as follows:

(a) Organize a sound system of preservative treatment and provide for the enforcement of standards;

(b) Standardize dimensions and tolerances and refuse to purchase timber that does not conform to these;

(c) Adopt a system of grading and an appropriate timber design code. AS 1720, Timber Engineering Code, is an excellent, flexible code that can be used in tropical countries;

(d) Concentrate at first on simple bulk products, e.g. stud frame walls or trussed rafter systems, to demonstrate economical construction using high quality timber.

UNIDO GENERAL STUDIES SERIES

The following publications are available in this series:

Title	Symbol	Price (US$)
Planning and Programming the Introduction of CAD/CAM Systems A reference guide for developing countries	ID/SER.O/1	25.00
Value Analysis in the Furniture Industry	ID/SER.O/2	7.00
Production Management for Small- and Medium-Scale Furniture Manufacturers A manual for developing countries	ID/SER.O/3	10.00
Documentation and Information Systems for Furniture and Joinery Plants A manual for developing countries	ID/SER.O/4	20.00
Low-cost Prefabricated Wooden Houses A manual for developing countries	ID/SER.O/5	6.00
Timber Construction for Developing Countries Introduction to wood and timber engineering	ID/SER.O/6	20.00
Timber Construction for Developing Countries Structural timber and related products	ID/SER.O/7	25.00
Timber Construction for Developing Countries Durability and fire resistance	ID/SER.O/8	20.00
Timber Construction for Developing Countries Strength characteristics and design	ID/SER.O/9	25.00
Timber Construction for Developing Countries Applications and examples	ID/SER.O/10	20.00
Technical Criteria for the Selection of Woodworking Machines	ID/SER.O/11	25.00
Issues in the Commercialization of Biotechnology	ID/SER.O/13	45.00
Software Industry Current trends and implications for developing countries	ID/SER.O/14	25.00
Maintenance Management Manual With special reference to developing countries	ID/SER.O/15	35.00
Manual for Small Industrial Businesses Project design and appraisal	ID/SER.O/16	25.00

Forthcoming titles include:

Design and Manufacture of Bamboo and Rattan Furniture	ID/SER.O/12	

Please add US$ 2.50 per copy to cover postage and packing. Allow 4-6 weeks for delivery.

ORDER FORM

Please complete this form and return it to:

UNIDO Documents Unit (F-355)
Vienna International Centre
P.O. Box 300, A-1400 Vienna, Austria

Send me _____ copy/copies of _____

_____ (ID/SER.O/_____) at US$ _____ /copy plus postage.

PAYMENT

☐ I enclose a cheque, money order or UNESCO coupon (obtainable from UNESCO offices worldwide) made payable to "UNIDO".

☐ I have made payment through the following UNIDO bank account: CA-BV, No. 29-05115 (ref. RB-7310000), Schottengasse 6, A-1010 Vienna, Austria.

Name _____

Address _____

Telephone _____ Telex _____ Cable _____ Fax _____

Note: Publications in this series may also be obtained from:

Sales Section
United Nations
Room DC2-0853
New York, N.Y. 10017, U.S.A.
Tel.: (212) 963-8302

Sales Unit
United Nations
Palais des Nations
CH-1211 Geneva 10, Switzerland
Tel.: (22) 34-60-11, ext. Bookshop

✂

ORDER FORM

Please complete this form and return it to:

UNIDO Documents Unit (F-355)
Vienna International Centre
P.O. Box 300, A-1400 Vienna, Austria

Send me _____ copy/copies of _____

_____ (ID/SER.O/_____) at US$ _____ /copy plus postage.

PAYMENT

☐ I enclose a cheque, money order or UNESCO coupon (obtainable from UNESCO offices worldwide) made payable to "UNIDO".

☐ I have made payment through the following UNIDO bank account: CA-BV, No. 29-05115 (ref. RB-7310000), Schottengasse 6, A-1010 Vienna, Austria.

Name _____

Address _____

Telephone _____ Telex _____ Cable _____ Fax _____

Note: Publications in this series may also be obtained from:

Sales Section
United Nations
Room DC2-0853
New York, N.Y. 10017, U.S.A.
Tel.: (212) 963-8302

Sales Unit
United Nations
Palais des Nations
CH-1211 Geneva 10, Switzerland
Tel.: (22) 34-60-11, ext. Bookshop